Journey to English 2

CARINA GUINAME SHIROMA
MAURICIO SHIROMA

© Text: Carina Guiname Shiroma and Mauricio Shiroma
© Design and illustration: Macmillan do Brasil 2012

Executive managing editor: Wilma Moura
Editors: Andréa Vidal and Isabel Lacombe
Assistant editor: Ana Carolina de Castro Gasonato
Language consultant: Robert C. Garner
Teacher's guide collaborator: Vitor Sugita
Proofreader: Maria Cecilia Jorgewich Skaf
Translators: Amini Rassoul, Anthony Doyle, and Maria Cecilia Jorgewich Skaf
Permissions coordinator: Fernando Santos
Minidictionary editor: Ana Carolina de Castro Gasonato

Concept design and page make-up by: Maps World Produções Gráficas
Design editor: Jorge Okura
Cover concept and design: Alexandre Tallarico
Concept design: Alexandre Tallarico and Carolina de Oliveira
Page make-up: Alexandre Tallarico, Carolina de Oliveira, and Vivian Trevizan
Proofreader: Ana Cristina Mendes Perfetti

Illustrator: Sidney Meireles (Giz de Cera)

Audio recording, mixing, and mastering: Maximal Studio
DVD illustrations, animations, infographs, software, and website: Maximal Studio

Dados Internacionais de Catalogação na Publicação (CIP)
(Câmara Brasileira do Livro, SP, Brasil)

Shiroma, Carina Guiname
　Journey to English / Carina Guiname Shiroma, Mauricio Shiroma. -- 1. ed. -- São Paulo : Macmillan, 2012.

　Manual do professor.
　ISBN 978-85-7418-863-8 (v. 1, inglês)
　ISBN 978-85-7418-870-6 (v. 1, português)
　ISBN 978-85-7418-865-2 (v. 2, inglês)
　ISBN 978-85-7418-871-3 (v. 2, português)
　ISBN 978-85-7418-867-6 (v. 3, inglês)
　ISBN 978-85-7418-872-0 (v. 3, português)
　ISBN 978-85-7418-869-0 (v. 4, inglês)
　ISBN 978-85-7418-873-7 (v. 4, português)

　1. Inglês (Ensino fundamental) I. Shiroma, Mauricio. II. Título.

12-06866　　　　　　　　　　　　　　CDD-372.652

Índices para catálogo sistemático:
1. Inglês : Ensino fundamental 372.652

Macmillan do Brasil
Rua José Félix de Oliveira, 383 – Granja Viana
06708-645 – Cotia – SP – Brasil
www.macmillan.com.br
elt@macmillan.com.br

Impresso no Brasil
EGB Gráfica - outubro/2014

Caro aluno,

Você já deve ter ouvido que "toda jornada começa com o primeiro passo", não é? Pois o primeiro passo da nossa jornada foi dado há muito tempo, quando nós tínhamos a sua idade e começamos a estudar inglês.

Quando embarcamos nessa viagem que é aprender uma nova língua, tínhamos os sonhos de todos os viajantes: visitar lugares distantes, conhecer pessoas incríveis, entender o que o mundo fala e conseguir nos comunicar com ele. Porém, naquela época, antes das maravilhas e facilidades tecnológicas que você conhece hoje, a jornada era bastante difícil: havia muitos obstáculos e poucos atalhos.

As dificuldades deixavam a jornada mais lenta, mas nem por isso menos interessante.

O segredo de todo bom viajante é saber se adaptar ao ritmo que cada trecho impõe. Em alguns trechos, viajamos na velocidade da luz; em outros, nos deixamos levar pela maré calma. Além disso, como em toda jornada, havia muitos caminhos à frente, e saber escolher o melhor deles fazia parte do desafio de chegar. Apesar de o destino ter sido o objetivo final da jornada, saber aproveitar as delícias do percurso foi, sem dúvida, o que mais nos encantou.

"Mas eles chegaram aonde?", você deve estar se perguntando.

Chegamos aqui, agora. E já podemos traçar o caminho para você, que está dando aquele primeiro passo rumo à mesma jornada de aprender uma língua.

Este livro é um mapa da jornada para você; use-o, transforme-o, descubra novos caminhos e possibilidades. Compartilhe as experiências com outros viajantes e divirta-se sempre.

Que você faça uma excelente viagem!

Carina e Mauricio

Know your book

Unit sections

Opening
The pictures in the opening pages of each unit are intended to stimulate impressions, feelings, and reactions, and lead to reflection on the theme.

Itinerary
Itinerary introduces the contents explored in each unit. This section allows you to evaluate what you already know and get ready / prepare yourself for what you will learn.

Reading
In the reading activities, you analyze and interpret different texts and learn strategies to make reading easier and more enjoyable. This section provides not only basic reading comprehension tasks, but also topics for reflection and discussion which will contribute to your education as a critical citizen.

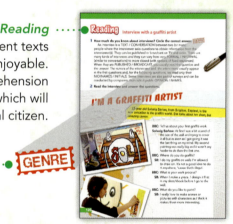

This icon indicates activities that focus on the characteristics of the text genre studied.

This icon indicates that the question(s) can only be answered by using logical deduction along with the information in the text.

Your Take
In these activities, you give your opinion and share ideas with classmates about the topics explored in the unit.

Listening
In this section, you listen to a great variety of oral genres. The activities use strategies that make listening easier.

This icon indicates that the activity provides practice in understanding the gist of the text.

This icon indicates that the activity practices comprehension of specific and detailed information from the text.

By the Way
This section provides comments about language and culture to expand and contextualize the different topics in the unit.

Speaking
In this section you learn how to gradually communicate in English in daily situations through conversation activities, – from the most simple, such as making suggestions, to the most complex, such as making a speech in class.

Vocabulary
In this section, you learn the meaning and pronunciation of words and expressions, which will expand your possibilities of communication in English. The section also helps you organize your knowledge.

Grammar
In this section, you are exposed to grammar within a communicative context to facilitate understanding. The activities help you analyze the patterns of language and draw conclusions about its rules. With this material, you learn how to use grammar both to produce and to understand oral and written texts.

Pronunciation
Pronunciation works as a support for the speaking and oral comprehension activities. This section contains dialogs, visual aids, and phonetic symbols to make you feel more confident and become more efficient in oral communication.

5

Writing

Writing is seen as a process. Here you learn how to use different resources to plan, outline, revise, and edit so you can write with autonomy. The genres you will produce will be shared with different audiences and published in different media.

Proofreading Tip

These boxes provide practical production, revision, and editing tips for you to gradually achieve autonomy in the writing process.

Road to Success

This section helps develop learner autonomy in general by providing several strategies, techniques, and tips for you to succeed in learning English.

Crossroads

Here you use English to learn, expand, or review contents from other school subjects.

Reflect

In this section, you think over the activities and texts in order to develop a critical sense. It encourages your personal engagement as a citizen.

This icon tells you that there is an activity on the DVD-ROM. When you see this symbol, go to page 166 and find the objectives, description, and tips to do the activity.

Extras

Looking Back

At the end of each unit, this self-evaluation tool will help you develop autonomy in learning English. Here you reflect on whether you have reached the goals established or still need more revision. You will also find suggestions for further study, such as websites, other resources in this book, and other useful titles.

Stopover

Every two units, you stop to review the content with fun and relaxing activities. This section will allow you to evaluate yourself and improve your knowledge in an enjoyable way.

6

Review
Every four units, you have a systematic, comprehensive review. You can test your knowledge and judge whether you need to practice more or not.

Grammar Reference
All the knowledge built in class is systematized in this section. It works as reference to study and review grammar.

Minidictionary
This is a bilingual dictionary with all the key words introduced in each book. Organized in alphabetical order, it provides the translation of the word or expression, the phonetic transcription, the word frequency, the word class, and examples of use.

Project
Every two units there is a project involving research, planning, preparation, and presentation. It is an opportunity to put English into practice in real contexts both inside and outside of school.

Extra Reading
Every two units, there is an extra text to develop reading skills. The texts are authentic and accompanied by activities that provide more practice for you to feel comfortable when reading.

A ⇄ B
For some conversation practices, there are special activities that can only be done with the exchange of information between two students. The section simulates a situation that is common in our daily speech – the search for information.

7

Contents

A day in the life — page 12

UNIT 1

- 14 **Reading** A school schedule
- 15 **Vocabulary** Routine activities & time
- 18 **Grammar** Simple Present (affirmative and negative – *I, you, we, they*)
- 20 **Pronunciation** Linking words
- 20 **Speaking** Finding differences and similarities
- 21 **Listening** A welcome speech
- 21 **Road to Success** Make your own picture dictionary
- 22 **Crossroads** Social sciences: time management
- 23 **Writing** Weekly schedule

The haves and have-nots — page 24

UNIT 2

- 26 **Reading** Description: *Where children sleep*
- 28 **Crossroads** Consumerism: experiences or material possessions
- 30 **Vocabulary** Life experiences & material possessions
- 31 **Speaking** Reacting with surprise
- 31 **Road to Success** From words to combination of words to sentences
- 32 **Listening** Public service announcement (PSA)
- 33 **Grammar** Simple Present (affirmative and negative – *he, she, it*)
- 34 **Pronunciation** Third person singular
- 35 **Writing** A new version of *Where children sleep*

36 **Stopover units 1&2**   38 **Extra reading 1**   40 **Project 1**

Breakfast of champions — page 42

UNIT 3

- 44 **Reading** Article: "Ready, set, breakfast!"
- 46 **Vocabulary** Breakfast food
- 47 **Pronunciation** The word *of*
- 48 **Grammar** Simple Present (interrogative: yes / no questions & short answers)
- 50 **Crossroads** Science: cheese & bacteria
- 51 **Listening** Cooking show
- 52 **Speaking** Offer, accept, and refuse food
- 52 **Road to Success** Variety of subjects
- 53 **Writing** Breakfast shopping list

What's that smell? — page 54

UNIT 4

- 56 **Reading** An advice column
- 58 **Vocabulary** Good hygiene
- 60 **Listening** A radio commercial
- 61 **Crossroads** History: dental hygiene in the past
- 63 **Pronunciation** Compound nouns
- 63 **Grammar** Adverbs and expressions of frequency
- 64 **Speaking** Expressing disgust
- 65 **Road to Success** Mental hygiene
- 65 **Writing** A survey about hygiene habits

66 **Stopover – Units 3&4**   70 **Project 2**   74 **Review – Units 1 to 4**
68 **Extra Reading 2**   72 **Looking Back at Units 1 to 4**

8

Yes, we can! page 76

- 78 **Reading** Charts
- 80 **Vocabulary** Body tricks
- 81 **Grammar** Can; possessive adjectives
- 83 **Crossroads** Math: percentages
- 84 **Writing** Chart: body tricks
- 85 **Speaking** Challenge your friends!
- 86 **Listening** Ask a scientist
- 87 **Pronunciation** Tongue twisters
- 87 **Road to Success** Body language

Manners page 88

- 90 **Reading** A handbook page: good manners in public
- 92 **Vocabulary** Manners
- 93 **Road to Success** Communication manners
- 94 **Listening** Subway announcements
- 95 **Crossroads** Citizenship: good manners in society
- 96 **Grammar** Imperative
- 98 **Speaking** Polite requests
- 98 **Pronunciation** Intonation in yes / no questions
- 99 **Writing** A thank-you note

100 **Stopover – Units 5&6**   102 **Extra Reading 3**   104 **Project 3**

Hello? page 106

- 108 **Reading** Instructions manual
- 110 **Vocabulary** Telephoning
- 111 **Listening** Telephone conversations
- 112 **Speaking** Cell phone calls
- 113 **Grammar** Present Continuous
- 115 **Pronunciation** Contractions – verb *to be*
- 115 **Road to Success** Telephoning strategies
- 116 **Crossroads** Geography: recycling electronics
- 117 **Writing** Instructions to use a cell phone

Art is everywhere page 118

- 120 **Reading** Interview with a graffiti artist
- 122 **Vocabulary** Arts
- 123 **Listening** An exhibition
- 124 **Crossroads** Arts: graffiti writing
- 126 **Writing** Identification label for your graffiti signature
- 126 **Road to Success** Arts help memorization
- 127 **Pronunciation** Emphasis
- 127 **Speaking** Opinions
- 128 **Grammar** Yes / no questions vs. wh- questions

130 **Stopover – Units 7&8**   134 **Project 4**   138 **Review – Units 5 to 8**
132 **Extra Reading 4**   136 **Looking Back at Units 5 to 8**

EXTRAS

- 140 **Grammar Reference**
- 148 **A ⇌ B**
- 149 **Minidictionary**
- 163 **Sites**
- 164 **Bibliography**
- 166 **DVD-ROM info**

9

Name: ....

School: ....

School address: ....

....

City: ....

State: ....

ZIP code: ....

School telephone number: ....

School email: ....

English teacher: ....

Class schedule

Monday	Tuesday	Wednesday	Thursday	Friday	Saturday

Test agenda

January	February	March	April	May	June

July	August	September	October	November	December

Classroom Language

UNIT 1 — A day in the life

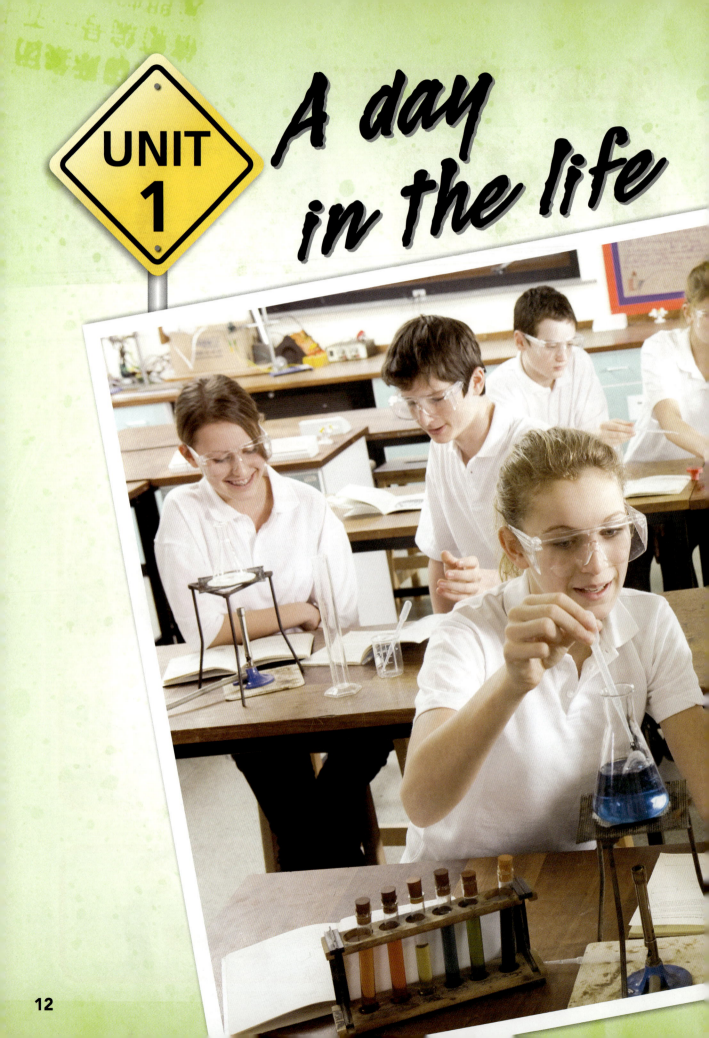

ITINERARY

In this unit, you will develop the following competences:
- reading a schedule to get general and specific information about a school routine;
- learning phrases and how to tell the time to talk about routine;
- using the Simple Present to describe routine;
- practicing linking words to connect sounds in sentences;
- using expressions to say if something applies to you or not;
- listening to a welcome speech to get general and specific information;
- making a picture dictionary to illustrate the words you learn;
- thinking about how you organize your time to develop time management skills;
- writing a weekly schedule to organize your time and activities.

 A school schedule

1 Complete the sentences with words from the box below.

> grades • weekdays • boarding school • weekend • boarders

a A .... is a school that has accommodations where students live. Students at a boarding school are called ....

b The ....: Monday, Tuesday, Wednesday, Thursday, and Friday.
The ....: Saturday and Sunday.

c The school years are called .... You are in grade 7.

2 Choose the correct alternative. GENRE

a A schedule is…
○ a list of things to buy.   ○ a list of activities.   ○ a list of friends.

b A schedule is organized by…
○ time.   ○ activity.

c The objective of a school schedule is to organize the .... activities and to inform .... about the students' routine.
○ parents' / the school   ○ students' / the parents   ○ students' / the students

A day in the life of a boarding school student

Weekday routine

6:45 am – Wake up and refresh
7:00 am – Sign-in to breakfast
7:40 am – Tidy up rooms
7:55 am – Off to class
8:00 am-3:00 pm – School day
3:00-4:00 pm – After-school sports or activities
5:30-6:30 pm – Dinner
6:00-7:30 pm – Prep time
7:00-8:30 pm – Computer lab open
9:00 pm – Grades 7 & 8 bedtime, lights out at 9:30 pm
9:30 pm – Grades 9 & 10 bedtime, lights out at 10:00 pm
10:30 pm – Grade 11 in their rooms, lights out at 11:00 pm
11:00 pm – Grade 12 in their rooms

Weekend routine

8:30 am-11:00 am – Cold breakfast
11:00 am-1:00 pm – Hot brunch
11:00 am – Boarders may sign out for the day
5:00-6:00 pm – Dinner
9:30 pm – On campus grades 7 & 8
10:00 pm – On campus grades 9 & 10
11:00 pm – Grades 7-11 students in their own rooms.
(lights out at 11:30) – Grade 12 students can be out until 12:00 with prior permission.

Adapted from QMS.bc.ca

3 Read the school schedule and write T (true) or F (false).

○ There are more activities on weekdays than on weekends.
○ One hour is the period of the after-school sports and activities.
○ On weekdays, bedtime is different for grades 7, 10, and 11.
○ On weekends, there are activities from 11:00 am to 5:00 pm.

4 From 8:00 am to 3:00 pm on weekdays, students have the "school day". What is it? {INFER}

....
....

YOUR TAKE

What's your opinion about studying at a boarding school? Explain!
....
....

Vocabulary   Routine activities

1 Listen and read the activities below. Then, look at the boarding school weekday schedule (page 14) and write the activity according to the time. 🎧 3

| go to bed | have dinner | have breakfast | wake up |
| go to class | use the Internet | play soccer | have classes |

6:45 am

7:00 am

7:55 am

8:00 am-3:00 pm

3:00-4:00 pm

7:00-8:30 pm

5:30-6:30 pm

9:00 pm

Unit 1 – A day in the life

2 Match the verbs with the nouns. Then listen and check your answers.

arrive the guitar

have  home

play  homework

do lunch

Time

3 Listen and read these examples.

eight oh five

eight o'clock

eight fifteen

eight thirty

eight forty-five

eight fifty-five

Alternatives
- **eight forty-five**: fifteen **to** nine
  (fifteen minutes to nine o'clock)
- **eight fifty-five**: five **to** nine
  (five minutes to nine o'clock)

Remember!
- 12:00 pm: midday
- 12:00 am: midnight

16

4 What time is it?

a **3:45**

It's three forty-five. / It's fifteen to four.

c **12:30**

It's ....

b **10:15**

It's ....

d **6:55**

It's ....

5 Write the time of your activities.
I wake up at *six thirty*.
- a I have breakfast at ....
- b I go to school at ....
- c I have lunch at ....
- d I do my homework at ....
- e I go to bed at ....

6 What time is it now?
It's ....

YOUR TAKE

Is your routine similar to the boarding school students' routine? What are the differences?

....
....
....
....
....
....
....
....

Grammar Simple Present – affirmative / negative

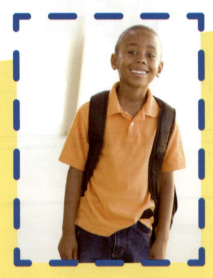

I **go** to school in the morning.
I **don't go** to school in the evening.

My brother and I **have** breakfast at home. (**We** have breakfast at home.)

My brother and I **don't have** breakfast at school. (**We** don't have breakfast at school.)

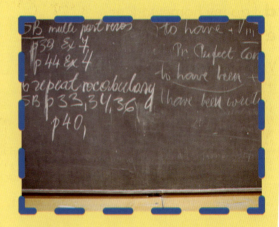

Classes **start** at 7. (**They** start at 7.)
Classes **don't start** at 8. (**They** don't start at 8.)

You **study** English at school.
You **don't study** Chinese at school.

1 Read the examples above again and answer.

  a In affirmative sentences with *I, you, we, they*, we use…
     ◯ verb.
     ◯ don't + verb.

  b In negative sentences with *I, you, we, they*, we use…
     ◯ verb.
     ◯ don't + verb.

2 Complete the paragraph with the **affirmative** or **negative** form of the verbs.

> have • play • go • watch • arrive • do

> My routine on Fridays is different. I wake up at 6:00 am and I don't have breakfast at home. I ………… to school and I ………… breakfast there. At 12:30 pm I ………… lunch. After lunch I ………… home; I go to my friend's house. We ………… basketball in the afternoon. After basketball practice, we ………… homework. At 4:30 pm we ………… music classes with a private teacher. I ………… home at 6:00 pm and ………… dinner with my parents. After dinner, they ………… TV; they prefer to play video games with me!

3 William and Nick are brothers. Read their daily routine. Compare with your routine.

Daily routine

6:00 am – wake up
6:30 am – breakfast
7:15 am – school
12:45 pm – arrive home
1:00 pm – lunch
2:00 pm – homework
5:30 pm – guitar lessons
7:00 pm – dinner
8:00 pm – Internet / games
10:00 pm – TV
11:00 pm – bed

I don't go to school at 7:15. I go to school at 7:00 am.

……………………………………………………………………………
……………………………………………………………………………
……………………………………………………………………………
……………………………………………………………………………
……………………………………………………………………………
……………………………………………………………………………
……………………………………………………………………………

Pronunciation — Linking words

When we speak English, we connect words and sounds and we don't stop between words.

1 Listen to the phrases below and repeat. 🎧 6

I wake up at six.

I go to school and I have breakfast there.

The classes start at seven.

What about you?

Speaking — Finding differences and similarities

1 Listen to the dialogs. 🎧 7

A: I wake up at <u>6 o'clock</u>.
What about you?
B: <u>Me too</u>.

A: I wake up at <u>6 o'clock</u>.
What about you?
B: <u>I don't</u>. I wake up at <u>6:15</u>.

2 Complete the column about you. Then talk to your partner to complete the friend's column.

Activity	My schedule	My friend's schedule
wake up		
have breakfast		
watch TV		
do homework		
have dinner		
go to bed		

Listening — A welcome speech

1 What do you know about welcome speeches? Match the parts of these sentences. GENRE

- **a** A welcome speech is…
- **b** Normally, the school principal is…
- **c** A good welcome speech is…
- **d** A welcome speech is…

- ○ always a positive message.
- ○ responsible for the welcome speech at a school.
- ○ presented on the first day of classes.
- ○ a message to say hello to a large group of people.

2 Listen to the welcome speech and check what the principal mentions. 🎧 8

- ○ His name.
- ○ The teachers' names.
- ○ The year.
- ○ The name of the school.
- ○ How the principal and the teachers feel.
- ○ The school schedule.
- ○ The opportunities and activities in the school.

> **REFLECT**
> In your opinion, why should a welcome speech have a positive message?

↑ Road to success

Make your own picture dictionary!

Um *picture dictionary* é um dicionário que explica as palavras através de fotos e ilustrações. Ele é muito útil para quem está aprendendo uma língua, pois ensina sem precisar de tradução e ajuda o leitor a memorizar as palavras através de imagens.

Crie seu *picture dictionary* a partir das palavras que você está aprendendo. Para isso:

- separe duas ou três páginas de caderno ou de um caderno novo para cada letra do alfabeto;
- recorte fotos de revistas e jornais velhos que ilustrem as ações que você aprendeu nesta unidade;
- organize as imagens em ordem alfabética, cole-as no caderno e, ao lado de cada uma, escreva a ação que representam.

Unit 1 – A day in the life

English  Crossroads Social Sciences

> A **quote** (or quotation) is a famous phrase or passage from a book, poem or play speech, etc., that is used to illustrate or support an opinion. It is important to mention the author of the quotation.

1 Read this quote and answer the questions.

> "The bad news is time flies. The good news is you're the pilot."
>
> Michael Altshuler – American motivational speaker.

a What is it about?
b Who is the author?
c What is the message of this quote?

How to organize your time

There are 168 hours in a week (24 hours per day, 7 days per week). Calculate the time you use for activities like: sleeping, eating, housework, exercise, transportation, homework, school, studying, and extra activities.

My typical week

Sleep	56 hours (8 hours per day)
Meals	21 hours (1 hour breakfast, 1 hour lunch, 1 hour dinner)
Housework	7 hours (walk the dog, make my bed, wash dishes…)
Exercise	5 hours (1 hour from Monday to Friday)
Transportation	5 hours (to go to school and go home)
Homework	5 hours (1 hour per day, from Monday to Friday)
School	25 hours
Total	124 hours

Subtract the total from 168 hours:
168 – 124 = **44 hours** (free time)

2 How much free time do you have per week?
I have .... hours free.

3 List other activities you like to do and your obligations too.

4 Organize these activities based on the free time you have.

Remember!

"Don't say you don't have enough time. You have exactly the same number of hours per day that were given to Helen Keller, Pasteur, Michelangelo, Mother Teresa, Leonardo da Vinci, Thomas Jefferson, and Albert Einstein." –
H. Jackson Brown (American author)

Writing — A weekly schedule

Preparing to write
1. Make a list of all your weekly activities.
2. Divide your activities by the days of the week.

Draft
3. Write your weekly schedule. Remember to:
   - divide it by time;
   - include your free time.

Proofreading
4. Proofread the spelling of the words.

Final version
5. Make a final version on your computer.
6. Post your schedule in your bedroom to memorize it.

Share
7. Print copies of your schedule and give them to your parents, grandparents, brothers and sisters. It's important that your family know about your activities and your free time.

Layout tip
Use different colors to highlight the different activities you do.

Go to *Looking Back* on page 72

UNIT 2
The haves and have-nots

Sherap is ten years old. He lives in a beautiful Tibetan monastery in Kathmandu, Nepal, and shares a room with seventy-nine other boys training to be monks. The boys all sleep in bunk beds and have very few personal possessions. Sherap's parents sent him there because it is believed that good luck comes to families who offer a son to the monastery. It also means they have one less mouth to feed.

Sherap has a long day. He gets up at 5:30 am to study, and he finishes the day with an hour of chanting at 9 pm. He eats 'dhal bhat' (rice and lentil soup), 'thukpa' (noodle soup), and 'roti' (flat bread). He admires his teacher and would like to be a 'kempo' martial arts teacher one day, but first he must finish school and then study privately for three years and two months.

MOLLISON, James. *Where children sleep.*

	Maria	Sherap
Age		
Lives in…		
Lives with…		
Has…		

6 Write *possibly* or *possibly not*. Explain. **INFER**

a Maria celebrates Mexican holidays.

....

b Maria likes studying a lot.

....

c Sherap eats all kinds of food, including beef and chocolate.

....

d Sherap's teacher is a martial arts teacher.

....

YOUR TAKE

Maria and Sherap have very different realities:
Maria has her own private doorbell outside her room.
Sherap shares a room with 79 other boys.

What are the advantages and disadvantages of each situation?

Unit 2 – The haves and have-nots

27

English Crossroads Consumerism

Experiences or material possessions?

1 In your opinion, is happiness related to material possessions? Why not?

2 Consider the options of experiences and material possessions below. For each pair, choose the one you prefer to have.

○ a day at a water park with friends   or   ○ a pair of cool sneakers

○ concert tickets to see your favorite band   or   ○ a modern music player

○ a balloon ride   or   ○ a cool jacket

28

◯ an elephant ride   or   ◯ the latest cell phone model

◯ a trip with family and friends   or   ◯ a modern video game

3 Are there more experiences or material possessions in your choices? Why?

4 Read the text below.

Buying experiences, not possessions, leads to greater happiness

A new psychology study suggests that buying life experiences, not material possessions, brings more happiness for the consumer and people around them.

According to Ryan Howell, assistant professor of psychology at San Francisco State University, the study demonstrates that buying experiences (for example, eating out or going to the theater) makes you happy because they satisfy the need for social connections and vitality – a feeling of being alive.

Adapted from ScienceDaily.com

Now choose the best option.
According to the text, consumers that buy .... are happy because experiences make you feel .... and they are an opportunity to be with ....

a ◯ experiences – energetic – other people
b ◯ material possessions – energetic – consumers
c ◯ experiences – happy – yourself

5 Consider the material possessions in your choices in activity 2. Are they really essential for your happiness?

Vocabulary   Life experiences & material possessions

1 Complete with the verbs in the box. Listen and check your answers.

LIFE EXPERIENCES

ride • travel • spend • see • eat • buy • go

MATERIAL POSSESSIONS

.... a rock concert.

.... typical dishes.

.... to a famous city.

.... the day at a theme park.

.... on a safari.

.... a camel.

.... brand-name clothes.

.... a tablet PC.

.... a cell phone.

.... a digital music player.

.... a mini game.

.... cosmetics.

2 Write about life experiences and material possessions you want to have.
I want to <u>ride a camel</u>.

....
....
....
....

30

Speaking — Reacting with surprise

1 Listen and read. 🎧 10

A: I want to <u>ride a camel</u>!

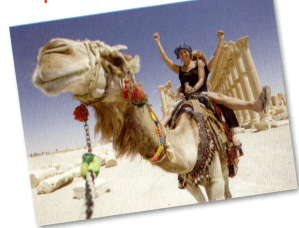

B: <u>Really? Me too!</u>   <u>No way! I prefer to go on a safari.</u>

2 Work with a partner.
Student A: Tell your sentences from activity 2 on page 30 to Student B.
Student B: Show surprise and respond.

↑ Road to success

words → combination of words → sentences

Agora que você já conhece várias palavras em inglês, comece a prestar mais atenção às combinações que pode fazer com elas.
Por exemplo, quantas combinações de palavras você consegue pensar para *ride*?

ride an elephant

ride a camel

ride a bike

ride a roller coaster

Anote no caderno ou em seu *picture dictionary* cada palavra nova que aprender, assim como as possíveis combinações que você conhecer. Peça ajuda ao seu professor ou consulte um dicionário, se achar necessário.
Saber as combinações corretas das palavras vai ajudá-lo a formar sentenças completas!

YOUR TAKE

Are there any toys, clothes, or electronics in your house that are not used often? Why? What can you do with these things?

Unit 2 – The haves and have-nots

31

Listening — Public service announcement

Public service announcements (PSAs) are messages broadcast on American television or radio for the benefit of society, such as donating blood and clothes, driving safely, keeping the city clean, etc.

1 Answer. `GENRE`

a The objective of a PSA is to…
- ○ convince people to buy new products.
- ○ convince people to participate in something.

b PSAs can be about…
- ○ an institution.
- ○ a cause.
- ○ new products.
- ○ a service.

c PSAs normally…
- ○ are long messages.
- ○ have a specific audience.
- ○ have clear and simple language.
- ○ are expensive to place on the radio or TV or in magazines or newspapers.

2 Listen to this PSA and mark the correct answer. 🎧 `SKIM`

What is the objective of this PSA?
- ○ To convince people to buy clothes.
- ○ To convince people to donate clothes.
- ○ To convince people to sell clothes.

3 Listen again and answer. 🎧 `SCAN`

a Chris, Tony, Lucy, and Erika are famous people.
○ True   ○ False

b "Clothes for People" is the name of the radio station.
○ True   ○ False

c The NGO gives clothes to homeless people.
○ True   ○ False

d What's the telephone number for "Clothes for People"?
....

Around 30% of the items donated cannot be sent to charity because they are not in a condition to be used, like torn clothes or single shoes.

From CampanhaDoAgasalho.sp.gov.br

32

Grammar   Simple Present - *he, she, it*

1 Read these sentences extracted from pages 26 and 27 and answer.

Maria lives in Mexico City.
She has one hour of homework every school night.
Sherap has a long day.
He gets up at 5:30 am to study.
It also **means** they have one less mouth to feed.
Maria **doesn't like** working hard.
She **does not watch** television very much.

a In affirmative sentences with *he*, *she* and *it*, we use…
  ○ *live, have, get, mean.*
  ○ *lives, has, gets, means.*

b In negative sentences with *he*, *she* and *it*, we use…
  ○ *doesn't* + verb.
  ○ *don't* + verb.

Attention!

Verbs ending in *-o*, *-ch*, *-sh*, *-x*, and *-z* add *-es*.
Maria go**es** to an American school.
She watch**es** Lucha Libre on TV.

Verbs ending in **consonant + -y** drop the *-y* and add *-ies*:
Sherap studi**es** every day at the monastery.

The verb *have* is **irregular**:
He **has** a lot of homework to do.

For the other verbs, we add *-s*.
She **plays** the guitar so well!
He **works** in the hospital.
Marcus **speaks** German and Russian.

Unit 2 – The haves and have-nots

2 Choose a verb from the box and complete the sentences about Maria and Sherap with the **affirmative** or **negative** form.

live • speak • play • go • have • like

a Maria .... to talk to her friends.

b Sherap .... English, but he speaks Nepali.

c Sherap .... his own room. He shares a room with 79 boys.

d Maria .... in a big house.

3 Read about Richard. Then, write sentences comparing you and him.

Name: Richard Gomez
Age: 12
Residence: New Jersey
School: Lorenzo Nunez Junior High
Languages: English and Spanish
Brothers / sisters: two sisters
Pets: cat
Music style: pop music

He lives in New Jersey. I live in Paraná.

....
....
....

Pronunciation Third person singular

1 Listen and match the verbs with the sounds. 🎧12

go**es**   /iz/
stud**ies**   /z/
lik**es**   /s/

Attention!
- In verbs ending with the sound of *p, t, k, f,* or *th*, the *s* sounds like /s/.
  stop, eat, work, proof, laugh
  stop**s**, eat**s**, work**s**, proof**s**, laugh**s**

- In verbs ending with the sound of *s, z, sh, ch, dj,* or *ks*, the *es* sounds like /iz/.
  dance, lose, wash, watch, judge, relax
  danc**es**, los**es**, wash**es**, watch**es**, judg**es**, relax**es**

- In verbs ending with other sounds, the *s* sounds like /z/.
  do, play, listen
  doe**s**, play**s**, listen**s**

2 Listen and write the verbs in the correct column. 🎧13

watches • lives • speaks • gets • eats • wants

/s/	/z/	/ɪz/

Writing — A new version of *Where children sleep*

Let's write a book about where the students in your class sleep.

Preparing to write
1. Read the descriptions on pages 26 and 27 again.
2. Copy the categories from the chart on page 34 and complete it with information about you.
3. Include other details in the chart. Examples: school activities, hobbies, etc.

Draft
4. Use the information in your chart to write about you.
5. To be in the book, your text needs to be in the third person. Rewrite it.

Proofreading
6. Revise the spelling, grammar (page 33), and punctuation.

Proofreading TIP
Use what you know.
Check if the verbs that talk about a third person have the *-s*.

Final version
7. Write a final version. Include a picture of yourself and your bedroom.

Sharing
8. Put all the texts and pictures together in the format of a book. Don't forget to make a front cover, a table of contents, and a back cover. Invite your teacher to write a preface for your book. Make copies to give to your parents, grandparents, and friends.

Go to *Looking Back* on page 72 ▶ **35**

Unit 2 – The haves and have-nots

Stopover Units 1 & 2

1 Find the verbs that go together with these words.

a .... to bed.
b .... classes.
c .... soccer.
d .... the Internet.
e .... home.
f .... homework.

2 Draw the clock hands.

a

eight ten

b

nine fifteen

c

one thirty

d

eleven forty-five
or
fifteen to twelve

e

three fifty-five
or
five to four

36 Units 1 & 2

3 Read the clues and write these kids' names.

Huey doesn't have a dog.

Yuri doesn't like sports, but he loves animals.

Robson doesn't have a cat.

Bruna and Sandra like flowers.

Bruna likes to talk to Huey. They are good friends.

Huey doesn't have pets.

4 Find out the verbs below and use the code to discover the name of Jamaica's national fruit. Clue: same letter, same number.

a She .... a lot of things in the morning.
           1   5   8   4

b Larry .... soccer matches on TV.
        11 12 6   7   3   8   4

c Louise never .... her hair.
             9   2 13 4   3   8   4

d Antonio .... English in another city.
          4   6 13 1 14 8   4

e Marcus .... two brothers.
          3 12 4

f Daniele .... with her mother.
         11 5   2 15 4

g Igor .... five languages!
      4 16 8 12 11 4

....
12   7 15 8   8

Stopover

Extra Reading 1

1 Read the lyrics to the song "Material things" by Avant. Then answer T (true) or F (false).

a ◯ This is a love song.
b ◯ His girlfriend is above all material things.
c ◯ Material things are his favorite things.
d ◯ To Avant, material things are nothing without his girlfriend.

Material things

by Avant

Lights, cameras, stars, crowds, noise,
After sets, cell phones, Internet, Vegas bets,
Private jets, limousine chauffeurs, all of that,
Money, clothes, and diamonds, cars, rims, shining
None of this compares to what I see in you

Materials don't mean a thing to me,
Girl you are the world to me,
If I had to pick a favorite thing,
It would easily be my baby

Materials don't mean a thing to me,
If I lost you lady, and I'd go crazy,
And I wouldn't have anything,
Black cars, fly homes, condos with the chefs,
Personal assistants, corporate, real estate,
Yachts that will take you far away to islands,
Whites wonder low, Costa Rica, Mexico,
Girl, none of this compares to what I see in you

Materials don't mean a thing to me,
Girl you are the world to me,
If I had to pick a favorite thing,
It would easily be my baby

Materials don't mean a thing to me,
If I lost you lady, and I'd go crazy,
And I wouldn't have anything
Loving without you, you make me wealthy,
I'm all about you, so special to me,

I turned off the phone, spent time alone
I don't want to be selfish, girl, you're the one
I put you above all the superficial things

Materials don't mean a thing to me,
Girl you are the world to me,
If I had to pick a favorite thing,
It would easily be my baby
Materials don't mean a thing to me,
If I lost you lady, and I'd go crazy,
And I wouldn't have anything

Materials don't mean a thing to me,
Girl you are the world to me,
If I had to pick a favorite thing,
It would easily be my baby,
Materials don't mean a thing to me,
If I lost my lady,
And I would not have anything

From SongLyrics.com

2 Avant mentions many items in the song. Classify them into the categories below.

cell phones • traveling to Las Vegas • private jets • limousines
sailing on a yacht • clothes • diamonds • cars • houses
traveling to Costa Rica • going to Mexico • meeting movie stars

Material things	Life experiences

Extra Reading 1

Project 1

A day in the life

It doesn't matter where you live, if you are 11, 12 or 13 years old and you are a student (from a boarding school or a regular school), you and all the other students in the world have very similar routines. But what about adults who are not students? Are their routines similar too?

1 The adults' routine depends a lot on what profession or job they have. Read about Steve Aldrin's life and routine.

A day in the life of Steve Aldrin

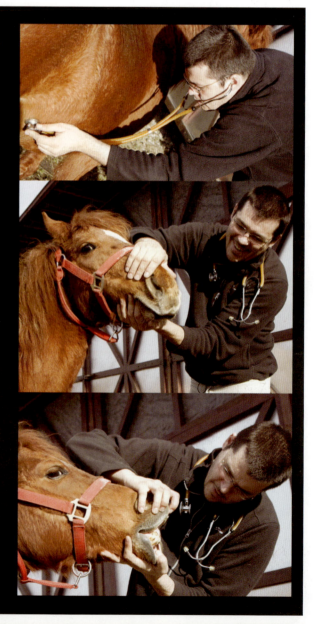

Steve Aldrin is a farm veterinarian. He lives in a farm in Kalispell, a city in the state of Montana, USA. He loves animals very much. He has four dogs, three cats, two horses, some pigs, and some cows in his farm. He has many patients and he loves his job.

Steve wakes up at 6 am and he has a big breakfast (bacon and eggs).

At 7:30 am he goes to the clinic and he checks his day schedule. During the day he visits his patients in the farms or helps his patients who come to the clinic. He arrives home at 5 pm and he has dinner with his wife, Monica. They watch comedy shows on TV or use the Internet and they go to bed at 11 pm.

2 Think of two adults you know. What are their names and their jobs? Use the dictionary, if necessary.

Name: ....
Job: ....

Name: ....
Job: ....

3 Talk to the two adults. Find out information about their lives and their routine. Use the phrases below to guide you and take notes.

	PERSON 1	PERSON 2
Where / live		
What / like (or don't like)		
Other information about his / her life		
What / do in the morning		
What / do in the afternoon		
What / do in the evening		
Times for breakfast, lunch, and dinner		
Other information about his / her work routine		

4 Take photos of the two people to illustrate their routine.

5 Write two paragraphs for each person. In the first paragraph, describe the person's life. In the second, talk about his / her routine.

....
....
....
....
....
....
....
....
....

6 Use your texts and the photographs to make a poster or a computer presentation to show to your classmates.

7 After you see your classmate's work, answer:
  a How many different jobs / professions are there, including all of your classmate's works? What are they?

  ....

  b Are the routines similar? What are the differences?

  ....

  c In your opinion, what jobs / professions are interesting? Why?

  ....

Project 1

UNIT 3
Breakfast of champions

ITINERARY

In this unit, you will develop the following competences:
- reading an article to get general and specific information about breakfast;
- learning vocabulary and the correct pronunciation of "of" to talk about what you have for breakfast;
- using the Simple Present to ask and answer questions about breakfast;
- reading about bacteria to learn more about cheese;
- listening to a cooking show to learn how to make ricotta;
- using expressions to offer, accept, or refuse food;
- develop the habit of learning about different subjects to learn new words and form opinions;
- writing a shopping list to remember what to buy.

Reading

An article: "Ready, set, breakfast!"

1 What do you know about articles? **GENRE**

a Match.

- An article is...
- The objectives of an article are...
- The elements of an article are...

- the headline, the lead, the body, and the conclusion.
- a written composition published in a magazine, newspaper, or on the Internet.
- to inform, to present research, to present an analysis, or to debate.

b Complete with the correct words.

summarize the ideas • title • subtitles • capture the attention

Elements of an article

The headline is the .... of the text.
The lead is the first paragraph of the text. The objective of the lead is to .... of the reader.
The body is the text. It can be divided into paragraphs or ....
The conclusion is the last paragraph of the text. The objective of the conclusion is to end or .... of the text.

c Read the article below. Identify the headline, the lead, the body, and the conclusion.

Ready, set, breakfast!

"Eat your breakfast. It's the most important meal of the day!"
Why do parents always say that?
Well, imagine you're a car. After a long night of sleep, there is no gasoline in your tank. Breakfast is the gasoline that gives you energy to go.

What do you need to eat?
Any breakfast is better than no breakfast, but try not to have croissants and cakes all the time. They're high in calories, sugar, and fat. They also don't contain the nutrients a person really needs.
Just like with other meals, try to eat a variety of foods, including:
- grains (breads and cereals)
- protein (meats, beans, and nuts)
- fruits and vegetables
- milk, cheese, and yogurt

Skipping breakfast
Some kids skip breakfast because they sleep too late or because they don't want to get fat. But skipping breakfast doesn't help people maintain a healthy weight. In fact, skipping breakfast makes you eat more calories during the day.

Do you still need to be convinced?

Just in case you need more evidence that eating breakfast is important, kids who don't eat breakfast have bad grades at school, get less iron (an important nutrient) in their diets, and have a higher body mass index (BMI), a sign they are overweight.

On the other hand, kids who eat breakfast do better in school, participate more in physical activities, and tend to eat healthy foods in general. So tomorrow morning, don't go to school on an empty stomach. Fuel up with a healthy breakfast!

Adapted from KidsHealth.org

2 What is the subject of the text? SKIM
- ◯ The importance of food.
- ◯ The importance of breakfast.
- ◯ The importance of weight.

Glossary

to skip: pular
weight: peso
overweight: acima do peso
fuel up: encher o tanque

3 Write T (true) or F (false). SCAN
- ◯ Croissants are high in calories, sugar, and fat.
- ◯ Nuts contain protein.
- ◯ You eat more during the day when you skip breakfast.
- ◯ Iron isn't an important nutrient.
- ◯ Students who don't eat breakfast have better grades.

4 Which of these foods don't contain the nutrients that we need? Read the text and check your answers.
- ◯ fruits
- ◯ croissants
- ◯ milk
- ◯ vegetables
- ◯ cakes

166

Body Mass Index measures the quantity of fat in your body through the formula [weight ÷ (height × height)]. The problem is that a muscular person and an overweight person may have the very same index. Nowadays scientists propose more realistic ways to measure the quantity of fat, such as the Body Adiposity Index which uses the measurement of the hip and height in the formula [hip ÷ (height × $\sqrt{\text{height}}$)] – 18.

Unit 3 – Breakfast of champions

45

Vocabulary Breakfast food

1 Listen and read the examples. 🎧14

a cup of coffee

a glass of orange juice

a slice of bread

a piece of cake

a banana

a bowl of fruit

2 Organize the words in the correct column. Then listen to check your work. 🎧15

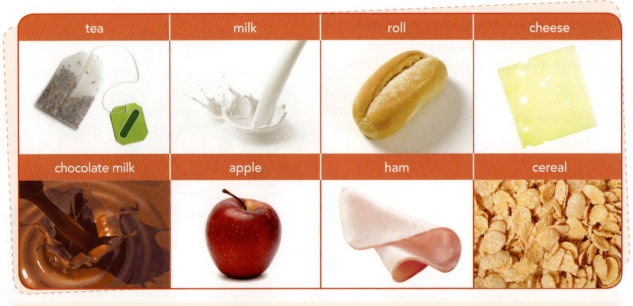

| tea | milk | roll | cheese |
| chocolate milk | apple | ham | cereal |

a cup of…	a glass of…	a / an…	a slice of…	a bowl of…

46

Traditional breakfast combinations

3 Complete the combinations and make sentences about your breakfast. Follow the example.

1. coffee + milk = coffee and milk
(like) I like coffee and milk for breakfast.
or
(don't like) I don't like coffee and milk for breakfast.

2. bread + butter = ... and ....
(eat) .... for breakfast.

3. crackers + jam = ... and ....
(like) .... for breakfast.

4. toast + eggs = ... and ....
(eat) .... for breakfast.

Pronunciation   The word *of*

1 Listen carefully. Do you hear the letter **f** in the word **of**?
- **a** a cup of coffee
- **b** a glass of orange juice
- **c** a slice of bread
- **d** a piece of cake
- **e** a bowl of fruit

Attention!
In general, the letter **f** in **of** is pronounced as /v/. Sometimes, the sound can disappear completely and only the letter **o** is pronounced.

2 Listen again and repeat the phrases.

Unit 3 – Breakfast of champions

47

Grammar

Simple Present – interrogative (yes / no questions) and short answers

1 Read what these people say about their breakfast.

Does she **like** chocolate milk?
No, she doesn't.
She prefers yogurt.

Do you **eat** ham?
Yes, I do! I love it!

Does it **contain** vitamin C?
Yes, it does.
Guava is rich in vitamin C and I have one every morning.

Do they **make** bread at home?
Yes, they do.

Hmm… **Do** we **like** this kind of food?
Yes, we do. It's Indian food.

2 Answer according to the examples.

  a In interrogative sentences with *I*, *you*, *we*, *they*, use…
    ◯ do + subject + verb.
    ◯ does + subject + verb.

  b In interrogative sentences with *he*, *she*, *it*, use…
    ◯ do + subject + verb.
    ◯ does + subject + verb.

  c In interrogative sentences, use *do* or *does*…
    ◯ after the subject.
    ◯ before the subject.

  d In short answers, use…
    ◯ subject + do / does.
    ◯ do / does + subject.

3 Complete the dialogs.

(he / put)
Does he put ricotta cheese in his sandwich?
Yes, he does. He loves ricotta cheese.

(he / put)
Does he put ricotta cheese in his sandwich?
No, he doesn't. He prefers mozzarella cheese.

a (you / make)

.... toasts for breakfast?
.... I prefer to eat crackers.

b (she / eat)

.... a banana for breakfast?
.... She eats a banana every morning.

c (they / have)

.... breakfast at school?
.... They have breakfast at home.

d (it / contain)

.... sugar?
.... This jam contains a lot of sugar.

4 Use the phrases below to ask your classmate about her / his breakfast habits. Then complete the table.

You: Do you <u>have breakfast every morning</u>?
Your classmate: <u>Yes, I do.</u>
You: Do you <u>drink a glass of milk for breakfast</u>?
Your classmate: <u>No, I don't.</u>

	Yes	No
have breakfast every morning	X	
drink a glass of milk for breakfast		X
have breakfast every morning		
drink a glass of milk for breakfast		
like crackers and jam		
drink a cup of tea in the morning		
eat a bowl of cereal in the morning		
eat fruits for breakfast		

Unit 3 – Breakfast of champions

49

English / Crossroads / Science

1 Answer the questions.
  a Do you like cheese?
  b Do you eat cheese every day?
  c What's your favorite type of cheese?
  d What's necessary to produce cheese?

bacteria
microorganisms (very small living things) that consist of only one cell.

  ○ milk   ○ salt
  ○ flour   ○ bacteria

2 What do you know about bacteria?
  a Where do you find bacteria?
     ○ On and in plants, humans, and animals.
     ○ On soil, in air and water.
     ○ In food.
     ○ In very hot and very cold places.
     ○ Everywhere.
  b Bacteria in food is always bad.
     ○ False   ○ True
  c Different cheese use different bacteria.
     ○ False   ○ True

3 Read and check your answers.

> **Bacteria and cheese**
>
> name   Kaley
> status student
> age   12
>
> Question – Are there different bacteria used to make different types of cheese?
>
> Answer – That's correct. The type of bacteria used to produce cheese determines the taste, so every cheese has its specific bacteria. In some cases, e.g., Roquefort, the kind of bacteria to make it is a well-kept secret.
>
> Available at Newton.dep.anl.gov

4 Do some research and answer these questions.
  a How do bacteria form holes in Swiss cheese?

  b How do bacteria make Limburger cheese so smelly?

Limburger cheese is very smelly.

Glossary

smelly: to have a bad smell

50

Listening — A cooking show

1 What do you know about cooking shows? **GENRE**

a A cooking show is a TV program that presents…
- ○ the production of industrialized food.
- ○ the preparation of food.
- ○ interviews with famous chefs.

b Mark true (T) or false (F).
- ○ The duration of a cooking show depends on the time necessary to prepare the food.
- ○ You have to be a chef to present a cooking show.
- ○ Cooking shows are for people who don't know how to cook.
- ○ The language used in a cooking show is very complicated.

2 Listen to the cooking show and cross out the items on the shopping list that are not necessary to make ricotta cheese. 🎧17

Shopping List
- 1 liter milk
- 6 eggs
- 1 bottle vinegar
- 1 bottle oil
- 1 kilo salt
- 1 bottle water

3 Listen again and order the directions from 1 to 5. 🎧17

Directions

- ○ Leave for 6 hours.
- ○ Boil milk.
- ○ Add vinegar and water. Mix.
- ○ Extract the water with a piece of cloth.
- ○ Your homemade ricotta is ready.

REFLECT
If it is so easy to make ricotta cheese at home, why do people prefer to buy it in supermarkets?

Speaking — Offer, accept, and refuse food

1 During breakfast, we sometimes offer or ask for food. Read and listen to the example. 🎧 18

Would you like **an apple**?

🙂 Yes, I'll have one, thanks!

🙁 Thank you but I'm not hungry.

Other ways to...	
accept	**refuse**
I'll have one, thanks.	Thank you but I'm not hungry / thirsty.
Sure! Thanks a lot.	I'm fine, thanks.
Thanks, I'm very hungry / thirsty!	Not now, thank you.

2 Practice the dialog with a classmate. Offer the food below.

a roll with ham and cheese

a piece of chocolate cake

toast with jam

a slice of ricotta cake

a glass of fruit juice

a cup of tea

↑ Road to success

Variety of subjects

É importante informar-se sobre assuntos diferentes para desenvolver conhecimentos gerais, aprender novas palavras e formar opinião. Você talvez não goste de cozinhar, e não queria saber como é feito o queijo, mas este conhecimento pode ajudá-lo a se expressar melhor, tanto no seu idioma nativo quanto na língua inglesa.

Pense nos assuntos que você conhece pouco ou não conhece (culinária, esportes, política, economia, ciências, etc.) e procure informar-se a respeito deles lendo jornais, revistas, páginas da internet ou consultando outras pessoas.

 Breakfast shopping list

Preparing to write
1. Go back to page 51 and read the shopping list again. Let's write a shopping list for a special breakfast.
2. In which occasions do you prepare a special breakfast? For whom?
3. What is the objective of a shopping list?
4. What information is necessary in a shopping list?

Draft
5. Make a list of things you like to have for breakfast. Use a dictionary if necessary.
   Remember: You have to read the shopping list, so use **good handwriting**.

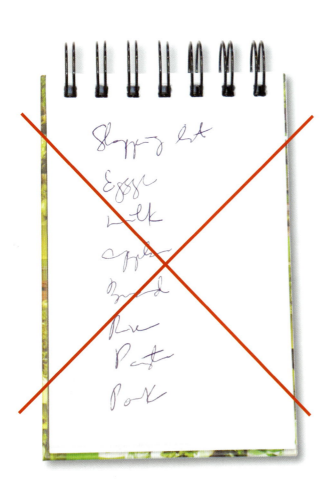
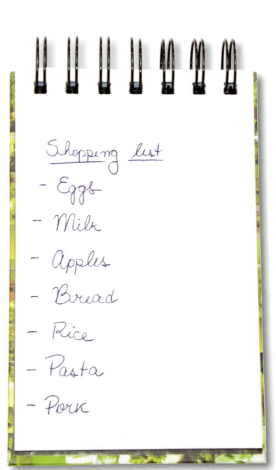

Proofreading
6. Check if all the items you want are on the list.
Note: In real life, it's not very important to check spelling, because the objective of the list is to help you remember.

Final version
7. Write your list on an appropriate piece of paper. Use good handwriting.

Go to *Looking Back* on page 73

ITINERARY

In this unit, you will develop the following competences:
- reading an advice column to get general and specific information about a hygiene problem;
- learning words, expressions, and their correct pronunciation to talk about hygiene;
- listening to a radio commercial to get general and specific information about a hygiene product;
- reading about ancient forms of hygiene to learn about the evolution of dental products;
- using adverbs and expressions of frequency to talk about habits;
- using expressions to show disgust;
- writing a survey to find out more about your classmates' hygiene habits.

Reading — An advice column

1 What do you know about advice columns? Write T (true) or F (false). GENRE

- ○ There are advice columns in magazines, newspapers, and on the Internet.
- ○ People write to advice columns because they need advice on personal problems.
- ○ The language in advice columns is usually informal.
- ○ People use real names in their letters because they want personal answers.
- ○ People that write the advice are famous.
- ○ The letters from the readers are sometimes very emotional.
- ○ The letters usually start with "Dear (name)".
- ○ Columnists are very emotional in their answers.

2 Match the underlined words with their category.

A Singular noun   **B** Plural noun   **C** Adjective   **D** Verb

- ○ One <u>foot</u>.
- ○ Two <u>feet</u>.
- ○ He <u>sweats</u> when it's hot.
- ○ Cotton <u>socks</u>.
- ○ <u>Shoes</u>.
- ○ This is a very <u>stinky</u> sneaker!
- ○ This place <u>smells</u> so bad!

56

Dear Heather,
I have stinky feet every time I remove my shoes. Even if I wear socks, my feet still smell bad. How can I make it stop?
                                    Rob

Rob
Stinky feet is a very common problem for people, so you don't have to feel bad about it.
According to the American Podiatric Medical Association, each foot has more than 250,000 sweat glands. Stress or dirt can make your feet sweat and smell even more, so it's a good idea to wash them regularly. But for many people, regular showers still don't solve the problem.
What you wear on your feet also affects how much they sweat and / or smell. Cotton socks and shoes that aren't made of vinyl or plastic are much better. Also, if you don't wear the same pair of shoes for two days in a row, they can air out and that's helpful to eliminate odor.
There are certain powders or remedies you can use to reduce foot odor. Of course, if your feet continue to smell after a few weeks, see a doctor to find out if there's another problem with them.
        Take care,
        Heather

Adapted from Gurl.com

3 Read the text and answer. **SKIM**
  a Who's Heather?
   ○ The person who needs help.
   ○ The person who gives advice.
  b What's Rob's problem?
   ○ He doesn't like socks.
   ○ He has stinky feet.

4 Read again and mark the true sentences. **SCAN**
   ○ Sweat causes foot odor.
   ○ Stress makes you sweat more.
   ○ Plastic shoes are good to reduce foot odor.
   ○ It's never necessary to see a doctor because your feet smell.

5 Look at the photos and answer: who has good habits to reduce or eliminate foot odor? Explain. **INFER**

I take a shower every day.

I never wear cotton socks.

I wear different shoes every other day.

Vocabulary Good hygiene

1 Complete these phrases with parts of the body. Then listen and check your work. 🎧19

  a Brush your ....   **b** Wash your ....

  c Clean your ....   **d** Wash your ....   **e** Wash your ....

2 Classify the actions below under the correct category. Then listen and check your work. 🎧20

Bite your nails.

Take a shower.

Wear clean clothes.

Wear dirty clothes.

Clip your nails.

Pick your nose.

GOOD HABITS	BAD HABITS

3 Complete these questions with the vocabulary from activities 2 and 3. Then ask the same questions to a partner.

Do you **clip your nails** in the morning?

a Do you .... in the morning?
b Do you .... at nights?
c Do you .... on Sundays?
d Do you like to ....?
e Do you ....?

59

Listening — A radio commercial

1 Listen to this radio commercial and answer. 🎧 21 [SKIM]
Which product is "Fresh Power Triple Action Plus"?

2 Listen again and answer. 🎧 21 [SCAN]

  a What does "Fresh Power Triple Action Plus" do? Mark all correct alternatives.

  ○ It kills bacteria.
  ○ It protects your feet.
  ○ It neutralizes the odor.
  ○ It cleans shoes and sneakers.
  ○ It leaves a fresh perfume for a day.

  b According to the commercial, "Fresh Power Triple Action Plus" is…
  ○ 50% more efficient.
  ○ 25% more efficient.
  ○ 35% more efficient.

  c Is it OK to use it on your feet?
  ○ Yes. It is 100% natural and can be used directly on your feet.
  ○ No. It is not safe for children and adults.

60

Crossroads: History / English

Dental hygiene in the past

1 Mark the dental hygiene products you use every day.

- ◯ dental floss
- ◯ toothpaste
- ◯ toothbrush
- ◯ mouthwash
- ◯ toothpick
- ◯ tongue scraper

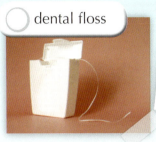
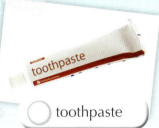

166

2 Is it possible to substitute those products with others?

3 Read about things people used for dental hygiene in the past and order the events in the timeline on the next page.

The toothbrush appeared around 3500 BC and was used by Egyptians and Babylonians. People chewed on one end of the stick until the fibers of the wood formed a brush.
From Gargles.net

The bristle brush was probably invented by the Chinese and brought to Europe during the seventeenth century.
From DiscoveriesInMedicine.com

These objects were used by Romans. The four objects at the top and the two bird-shaped ones are toothpicks.
From BritishMuseum.org

Marks from dental floss have been found in the teeth of early pre-humans and American Indians.
From Abc.net.au

Early Egyptian, Chinese, Greek, and Roman writings describe numerous mixtures for both pastes and powders. The more appetizing ingredients included powdered fruit, burnt shells, talc, honey, ground shells, and dried flowers. The less appetizing ingredients included mice, the head of a hare, lizard livers, and urine. Powder and paste formulas continued to multiply through the Middle Ages.
From DiscoveriesInMedicine.com

Ancient Greek recipe for mouthwash: "leaves of the olive tree, milk, the juice of pickled olives, gum myrrh with wine and oil, pomegranate peelings, nutgalls, and vinegar."
From DocShop.com

BY THE WAY... The word **hygiene** comes from the Greek word *hygies*, which means 'healthy'.

A. The first toothbrush appears.
B. The bristle brush arrives in Europe.
C. Many dental powder and paste formulas appear.
D. Evidences of the use of dental floss.

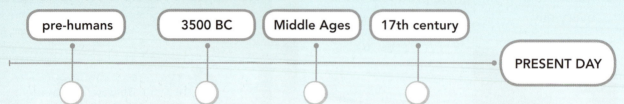

pre-humans   3500 BC   Middle Ages   17th century   PRESENT DAY

4 Match the ingredient with the product.

A mouthwash   B pastes and powders

○ wine

○ mice

○ hare

○ pomegranate

REFLECT
Is it important to know the ingredients of the dental products you use? Why (not)?

Pronunciation — Compound nouns

A **compound noun** is a noun formed by two words. The words can be written together (tooth + brush = toothbrush) or separated (tongue + scraper = tongue scraper).

1 Listen to the compound nouns and pay attention to their pronunciation. Then listen again and repeat. Notice that the stress is always on the first word. 🎧22

> **tooth**brush • **tongue** scraper • **tooth**paste
> **mouth**wash • **tooth**pick • **foot** powder

Grammar — Adverbs and expressions of frequency

1 Look at the chart, read the sentences and answer the questions.

Activity	M	T	W	T	F	S	S
brush teeth	✓	✓	✓	✓	✓	✓	✓
floss teeth		✓		✓		✓	
use mouthwash	✓					✓	
use a tongue scraper			✓				
use a toothpick							

> To ask questions about frequency, we use **how often**:
>
> **How often** do you brush your teeth?

I **always** brush my teeth. (I brush my teeth **every day**.)
I **often (frequently)** floss my teeth. (I floss my teeth **three times a week**.)
I **sometimes** use mouthwash. (I use a mouthwash **every other day/twice a day**.)
I **rarely** use a tongue scraper. (I use a tongue scraper **once a week**.)
I **never** use a toothpick.

2 The words in blue come…
   ◯ before the verb.
   ◯ after the verb.

3 The words in green are…
   ◯ at the beginning of the sentence.
   ◯ at the end of the sentence.

4 Write the adverbs in order of frequency.

> sometimes • always • rarely • never
> • often/frequently

5 Write the expressions in order of frequency.

> every day • every other day • twice a month
> • three times a month • once a month

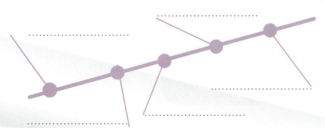

Unit 4 – What's that smell?

63

6 Look at this chart and answer the questions.

Activity	M	T	W	T	F	S	S
clip her nails			✓				✓
wear dirty socks							
use foot powder in her shoes					✓		
wash her hair	✓		✓		✓		
take a shower	✓	✓	✓	✓	✓	✓	✓

a How often does she clip her nails?
....
b How often does she wear dirty socks?
....
c How often does she use foot powder in her shoes?
....
d How often does she wash her hair?
....
e How often does she take a shower?
....

Speaking Expressing disgust

1 When we see or talk about bad habits, it's natural to react with disgust. Listen and read an example. 🎧23

Chad: My dog drinks water from the toilet.
Debra: Eww!

Other ways to express disgust
Gross!
Yuck!
That's disgusting!

2 Work with a partner.
Student A: Form sentences about bad habits. Talk to your partner.
Student B: Express disgust.

a  (not / take a shower every day)

d  (wear dirty socks)

b  (pick her nose)

e 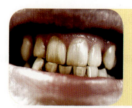 (not / brush his teeth every day)

c  (wear stinky clothes)

f  (not / clip her nails)

⬆ Road to success

Mental hygiene

Quando falamos em higiene, devemos lembrar que ela não se aplica apenas ao nosso corpo. Uma boa higiene mental nos ajuda a lidar melhor com o que acontece à nossa volta e, consequentemente, a viver melhor.

Atividades como conversar com os pais e os amigos, ouvir música, ler bons livros, assistir a filmes, assistir ou praticar esportes, passear ou cuidar dos animais de estimação podem contribuir para manter uma boa higiene mental.

Writing — A survey about hygiene habits

Preparing to write

A survey is a questionnaire to investigate something. You want to investigate if your classmates have good hygiene habits.

1. Make a list of 5 topics about which you want to ask your classmates.
   Ex.: *brush teeth.*
2. For each topic, write one question about hygiene habits.
3. Ask your classmates and take notes of their answers.

Draft

4. Write your classmates' answers in the form of sentences.
   Ex.: *Fifteen people in my class brush their teeth three times a day.*
5. Write your conclusion: do your classmates have good or bad hygiene habits? Why?

Final version

6. Write the final version of your survey. Include the sentences and the conclusion.

Share

7. Share your results with your classmates. Do you and your classmates have the same conclusions?

Proofreading TIP

Connectors can make your text better: Use *and* to join similar ideas in one sentence, *but* to join different ideas and *because* to explain a reason.
Ex.: *The students brush their teeth everyday, but they don't have good hygiene habits because they don't floss and never use mouthwash.*

Stopover Units 3 & 4

1 Match these photos and write.

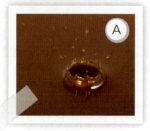

(1) + (A) = a cup of coffee

◯ + ◯ = a cup of tea
◯ + ◯ = a glass of chocolate milk
◯ + ◯ = a bowl of cereal

◯ + ◯ = a slice of ham
◯ + ◯ = a piece of banana
◯ + ◯ = a glass of milk

2 Find the way out of the labyrinth and form a sentence with the words you find on the way.

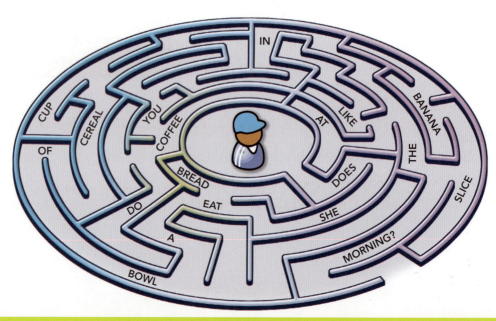

66 Units 3 & 4

3 Unscramble these adverbs of frequency.

a **MITOSESME** ....
b **LAYWAS** ....
c **LAYERR** ....
d **NERVE** ....
e **FENTO** ....

4 Substitute the faces with letters and complete these phrases.

You have to brush your .... every day. ....

Wash your .... before you eat. ....

Wash your .... after you get up. ....

Clean your .... regularly. ....

Wash your .... at least three times a week. ....

Stopover 67

Extra Reading 2

1 Do you like to read comics? What are your favorite characters?
....
....
....

2 Do you read Garfield's comics? What do you know about him? Complete the sentences.

  a Garfield is an orange .... and he lives with .... and .... (the dog).

  b He likes to ....
  ....
  ....

  c He doesn't like to ....
  ....
  ....

3 Read the comics and answer the questions.

From Garfield.com

Glossary

danish: a kind of sweet roll, normally filled with jam or nuts

  a Does Jon talk to Garfield?
  ....

  b Does Garfield answer Jon's questions?
  ....

68   **Extra Reading 2**

c What does Garfield want for breakfast?

d What does Jon serve Garfield for breakfast?

e Does Garfield like his breakfast?
....

f In the end Garfield says "people don't give cats any credits." What does he mean?
   ◯ People never understand what cats say.
   ◯ People don't respect the cats' opinions.
   ◯ People respect the cats.

Extra Reading 2

Project 2

Marketing a product

> When companies create a new product, the marketing department has basically three responsibilities:
> 1. Give a good name to the product;
> 2. Create a slogan for the new product;
> 3. Advertise the product on the radio, TV, magazines, etc.

1 Your company created a new product. What product is it?

◯ toothpaste   ◯ soap   ◯ shampoo   ◯ deodorant   ◯ mouthwash

2 Choose one or more scents or flavors for your product. Use a dictionary if necessary.

Flavors
- ◯ mint
- ◯ tutti-frutti
- ◯ strawberry
- ◯ cinnamon
- ◯ other: ....

Scents
- ◯ chocolate
- ◯ flowers
- ◯ lavender
- ◯ unscented
- ◯ other: ....

3 Creating a name for a product is not difficult. Choose two or three adjectives from the lists below, mix them and create a name for your product.

> super • extreme • plus • cool • extra • total • white
> clear • clean • fresh • herbal • natural • active • pure • organic

....
....
....

70   Units 3 & 4

4 Creating a slogan is a little more difficult. Choose one of the options of slogans below and change the underlined words with the words from activity 3 to adapt it for your product.

EXTREME COOL WHITE:
THE TOOTHPASTE OF YOUR LIFE.

NINE OUT OF TEN DENTISTS / DOCTORS RECOMMEND
Extreme Cool White Toothpaste.

You like
EXTREME COOL WHITE TOOTHPASTE.
Extreme Cool White Toothpaste likes you.

Get more from
EXTREME COOL WHITE TOOTHPASTE.

EXTREME COOL WHITE TOOTHPASTE
makes you happy.

Good things happen after
EXTREME COOL WHITE TOOTHPASTE.

5 List the qualities of your product.

○ it's antiperspirant
○ it eliminates odor
○ it gives you 24-hour protection
○ it eliminates germs and bacterias
○ it's 100% natural
○ it protects the .... (part of the body)
○ it treats the .... (part of the body)
○ other: ....

6 Create a radio commercial to advertise your product.

> **Remember!**
> • You learned that a radio commercial is a short message that uses voice messages, music, and sound effects to advertise a product.

Use the model below and adapt it. Change the underlined words and sentences with the information from activities 1 to 4.

Teenager: Eww. My <u>teeth</u> don't look very good.
Narrator: Are you protecting your <u>teeth</u>? Are you treating your <u>teeth</u> well? Are you sure? (pause) Stop having doubts, use <u>Extreme Cool White</u>! It <u>protects and treats your teeth and it is 100% natural</u>! <u>Extreme Cool White</u> is safe for adults and teenagers and it comes in two delicious <u>flavors: tutti-frutti and mint</u>.
Teenager: Mom, let's go to the supermarket. I need <u>Extreme Cool White</u> NOW!
Narrator: <u>Extreme Cool White</u>: the <u>toothpaste</u> of your life.

7 Record your radio commercial. Include sound effects and music. Then play it to your classmates.

Project 2   71

Looking Back at UNIT 1

Now I can...	😊 😕	Learn more about it:
read a schedule about a school routine.		
talk about routine and tell the time.		What time is it around the globe? Check it out at <www.timeanddate.com/worldclock>.
use the Simple Present.		Study the information on page 140 in the *Grammar Reference* section.
use linking words to connect sounds in sentences.		
say if something applies to me or not.		Read one or more books from the series *A day in the life (First facts: community helpers at work)*, by Heather Adamson.
listen to a welcome speech.		
organize my time.		Read the book *Organizing from the inside out for teenagers: the foolproof system for organizing your room, your time, and your life*, by Julie Morgenstern and Jessi Morgenstern-Colón. A must read for those who want to be more organized in their lives.
write a weekly schedule.		Create a weekly schedule online at <www.sealandserpent.org/schedgen/schedule generator.php>.
make a picture dictionary to illustrate the words I learn.		

Looking Back at UNIT 2

Now I can...	😊 😕	Learn more about it:
read an excerpt from a book about the lives of two teenagers.		Read the book *Where children sleep*, by James Mollison. It shows how children from different parts of the world live.
make smart choices considering experiences and material possessions.		Watch the movie *The Bucket List* (2007). It tells the story of a mechanic and billionaire both diagnosed with terminal cancer that decide to do everything they've always wanted, like go skydiving, drive a sports car, etc.
talk about life experiences and material possessions.		
react with surprise.		
form correct sentences.		
listen to a public service announcement about an NGO.		Check out the website <http://www.psaresearch.com/> and take a look at other PSAs.
use the Simple Present and the correct pronunciation of verbs to give general information about people.		Study the information on page 141 in the *Grammar Reference* section.
write a text to be used in a new version of a book.		

Looking Back

Looking Back at UNIT 3

Now I can...	😊 😟	Learn more about it:
read an article about breakfast.		
talk about what I have for breakfast.		Go to <www.cuisinenet.com/digest/breakfast/map_world.shtml> and find out what people around the world usually have for breakfast.
use the Simple Present to ask and answer questions.		Study the information on page 142 in the *Grammar Reference* section.
read about bacteria to learn more about cheese.		Learn more about home production of cheese at <www.dailymotion.com/video/xehqz2_how-to-make-homemade-cheese_lifestyle>.
listen to a cooking show to learn how to make ricotta.		Find recipes appropriate for you age in the book *Teens cook: how to cook what you want to eat*, by Meghan Carle, Jill Carle, and Judy Carle.
offer, accept, or refuse food.		
write a shopping list to remember what to buy.		Check out shopping lists from people in different parts of the world in *Milk eggs vodka: grocery lists lost and found*, by Bill Keaggy.
learn about different subjects to learn new words and form opinions.		

Looking Back at UNIT 4

Now I can...	😊 😟	Learn more about it:
read an advice column about a hygiene problem.		Read more advice columns at <http://www.askdrm.org>.
talk about hygiene.		Learn more words related to the body at <iteslj.org/v/ei/body.html>.
listen to a radio commercial about a hygiene product.		
read about ancient forms of hygiene to learn about the evolution of dental products		
use adverbs and expressions of frequency to talk about habits.		Study the information on page 143 in the *Grammar Reference* section.
show disgust.		
write a survey to find out more about my classmates' hygiene habits.		Find out more about keeping a healthy body in *The teenage human body operator's manual*, by Lee White, Caesar, Ph.D. Pacifici, and Mary Ditson.

Looking Back   73

Review Units 1 to 4

1 Phil is a robot collector. Order this conversation between Phil and Grace and mark **P** (for Phil) or **G** (for Grace).

- ○ They are great! Where do you buy them? ....
- ○ No, I don't. But I'd like to start a doll collection one day. ....
- ○ Really? Do you get many robots for free? ....
- ○ Do you have a favorite robot? ....
- ○ Yes. Do you like them? ....
- ○ I don't buy them in stores. People usually give them to me. ....
- ○ Is this your robot collection? ....
- ○ People know that I collect robots and they call me when they know of any robots available. ....
- ○ Oh, yes! I like these old robots from the 50s. They are very rare. Do you collect anything? ....

2 Andrea and Sammy play the guitar. They want to find a day to practice together. Complete their conversation with adverbs or expressions of frequency.

Sammy's schedule

	Monday	Tuesday	Wednesday	Thursday	Friday
morning	–	–	–	–	–
afternoon	help father at work	help father at work	help father at work	help father at work	help father at work
night	–	volunteer work (first week of the month)	–	dentist appointment	soccer practice

Andrea: Are you free on Tuesday at night?
Sammy: No, I have volunteer work ....
Andrea: What about Friday?
Sammy: I .... have soccer practice on Fridays. How about Wednesday? I .... do anything on Wednesdays.
Andrea: No, I have English classes on Wednesdays. What about afternoons?
Sammy: I .... have free time in the afternoon. I help my father at work ....
Andrea: I have Thursdays free.
Sammy: I .... have a dentist appointment on Thursdays.
Andrea: We are .... at school in the morning…
Sammy: Yes… wait, what about Mondays?
Andrea: Oh, yeah, Mondays! That's it!

74 Units 1 to 4

3 Complete this text about Karen and answer the questions.

Karen McNeil is a Scottish country dancer. She is not Scottish (she was born in Manchester, England), but she .... (like) to preserve the family traditions. There are rehearsals at her school on Fridays and she .... (practice) for about 3 hours. She .... (love) to dance to many types of music, but she .... (prefer) the "reel", which is the most popular folk dance in Scotland. She .... (dance) in groups of three or four people. Her mother .... (dance / negative) the reel, but she always .... (watch) and .... (encourage) Karen to keep dancing. Karen .... (know / negative) if she will always be a professional dancer, but she .... (know) she will always love it.

a Is Karen from Scotland?
....

b Where does she practice?
....

c When does she practice?
....

d Does she like to dance to other types of music?
....

e Does her mother dance too?
....

Review

UNIT 5
Yes, we can!

ITINERARY

In this unit, you will develop the following competences:

- reading an advice column to get general and specific information about a hygiene problem;
- learning words, expressions, and their correct pronunciation to talk about hygiene;
- listening to a radio commercial to get general and specific information about a hygiene product;
- reading about ancient forms of hygiene to learn about the evolution of dental products;
- using adverbs and expressions of frequency to talk about habits;
- using expressions to show disgust;
- writing a survey to find out more about your classmates' hygiene habits.

Reading Charts

A chart is a representation of information in the form of curves, columns, or graphs. To understand a chart, you have to read it in the correct order: title, horizontal line (or horizontal axis), vertical line (or vertical axis), and color codes.

1 Read the chart below and answer the questions.

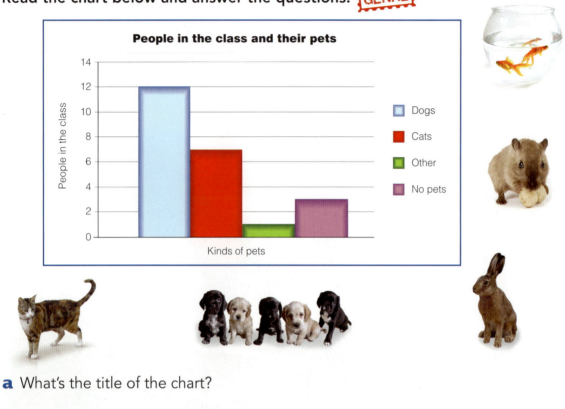

a What's the title of the chart?
....

b What does the horizontal line show?
....

c What does the vertical line show?
....

d What color represents "cats"?
....

e What does the blue column represent?
....

f What does the purple column represent?
....

g What are the conclusions of the chart? Write T (True) or F (False).

○ Dogs are very popular in the class.

○ Two people have pets that are not dogs or cats.

○ More people have dogs than cats.

2 Learn the words below before you read the text.

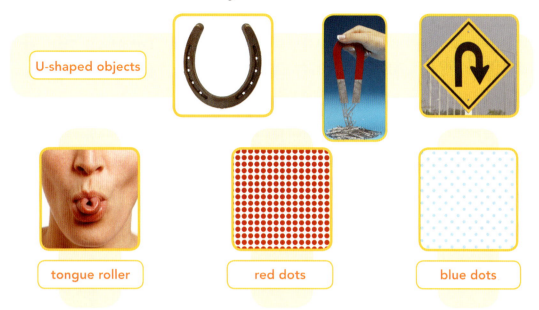

3 Read the chart from the American Society of Human Genetics and answer.
  a What's the title of the chart?
  b What does the horizontal line show?
  c What does the vertical line show?
  d What color represents "women"?
  e What color represents "men"?
  f What does the first column represent?
  g What does the second column represent?

Over 1,600 people visited the American Society of Human Genetics booth at the Festival Expo on the National Mall. We collected data from all visitors for the ability to roll the tongue into a U-shape. By the end of two days, we had collected an impressive dataset.

A European study in the 1940s noted that 70 percent of the population can roll their tongues and 30 percent cannot. Our data show a similar percentage. We can also see that blue and red dots are evenly distributed in both columns, showing that sex does not affect the tongue-rolling ability.

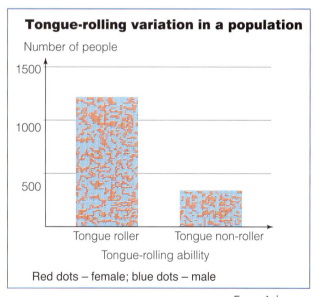

From Ashg.org

4 Now read about the study and answer T (true) or F (false).
  ◯ 1,600 people participated in the study in 2 days.
  ◯ The results are different from a study conducted in the 1940s.
  ◯ The ability to roll the tongue depends on the sex of the person.

Vocabulary Body tricks

1 Listen and read the names of some parts of the body. 🎧24

tongue

eyebrow

eyes

finger

2 Match the sentences to the pictures. Then listen and check your answers. 🎧25

a Roll your tongue.
b Raise your eyebrow.
c Touch your nose with your tongue.
d Wink with both eyes (right or left).
e Snap your fingers.
f Whistle with your fingers.

1

2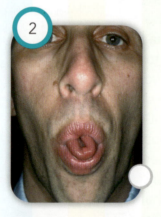

3

4

5

6

Grammar *Can*

1 Read these examples.
We use *can* to talk about abilities.

Can she roll her tongue?

Can he roll his tongue?

I **can** roll my tongue. You **can** roll your tongue too.

They **can't** roll their tongues.

Yes, she **can**.

No, he **can't**.

2 Answer the questions.

a The structure of affirmative sentences is…
- ○ subject + *can* + verb.
- ○ verb + *can* + subject.

b The structure of negative sentences is…
- ○ subject + *can't* + verb.
- ○ verb + *can't* + subject.

c The structure of interrogative sentences is…
- ○ subject + *can* + verb.
- ○ *can* + subject + verb.

d We use **can** with…
- ○ I, you, he, she, it, we, they.
- ○ I, you, we, they.
- ○ he, she, it.

3 Write sentences about body tricks that you *can* or *can't* do.

I can't wink with my left eye.

....
....
....
....

Unit 5 – Yes, we can!

81

Possessive adjectives

4 Interview your friends. Then complete the chart below with the quantities.

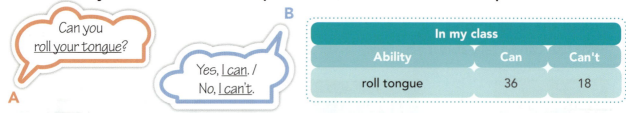

5 Write the results.

In my class, thirty-six people can roll their tongues and eighteen can't.

....
....
....
....
....
....

6 Learn the possessive adjectives and complete the sentences.

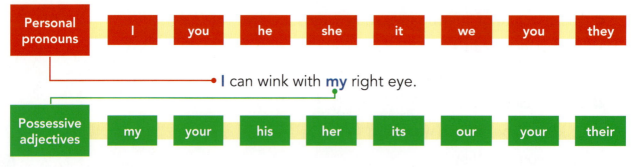

a I can whistle, but .... brother can't.
b You can't touch your nose with .... tongue, right?
c Jennifer has brown eyes. .... hair is brown too.
d Jennifer's friend, Mark, can do many body tricks. He can wink .... eye and roll .... tongue at the same time.
e My dog can touch .... nose with its tongue.
f The band members snap .... fingers when they sing.
g We are twin brothers. We can do the same body tricks with .... tongues.

1 Learn how to calculate percentages.

Percentage: a part of 100
(per cent = per hundred).

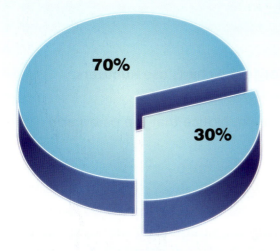

In a group of 100 people, 70 can roll their tongues and 30 can't roll their tongues. What does it mean in percentages?

> 100% = 100 people
> (in a group of 100 people)
> 70% = 70 people
> (in a group of 100 people)
> 30% = 30 people
> (in a group of 100 people)

In a group of 1,600 people, 480 can't roll their tongues.
What's the percentage of 480 in a group of 1,600? We can use cross multiplication to calculate that.

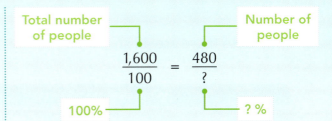

$$\frac{1{,}600}{100} \times \frac{480}{?}$$

multiplication

1,600 X ? = **1,600 ?**
100 X 480 = **48,000**

So:

1,600 ? = 48,000

Move 1,600 to the other side and divide:

$$? = \frac{48{,}000}{1{,}600}$$

The final result is:

? = 30

Conclusion: 480 of 1,600 = **30%** of the people.

2 Now you try!
In a class of 58 students, 28 are girls. Calculate the percentage of girls.

83

WRITING Chart – body tricks

Preparing to write

1. Go back to page 82, **activity 4**. Calculate the percentage of each *can* item. For example:

In my class there are 42 students.

In my class		
Ability	Can	Can't
roll tongue	27	15

42 = 100%

27 = 64,28%

2. Read the charts on pages 78 and 79 again. Notice the charts use **numbers**, not percentages.

3. Read about the study on page 79, **activity 4**, again. Notice that the paragraph talks about **percentages**.

Draft

4. Prepare a chart to represent the results of **activity 6** on page 82. Your horizontal line shows "Body tricks" and your vertical line shows "Number of people in the class".

5. Write sentences to illustrate the results. Use percentages.

6. Proofread your text.

Proofreading TIP
Don't use punctuation at the end of chart titles or axis titles.

Final version

7. Write a final version of your sentences and draw a final version of your chart.

Share

8. Post your charts on the wall of the class or school. Are your friends surprised by the results?

Speaking — Challenge your friends!

1 Listen and read. 🎧 26

I bet you can't <u>roll your eyes back</u>!

 Of course I can! Look!

You're right, I can't do that.

2 Practice the dialog with a classmate. Use the ideas below.

Student A: Challenge your friend.
Student B: Show you can do it or say you can't.

touch your feet

whistle *Happy Birthday*

roll back your eyes

calculate 15% of 467 in one minute

snap your finger with both hands

wink 20 times in 10 seconds

Unit 5 – Yes, we can!

85

Listening — Ask a scientist

1 Listen to Dr Hopper's answer and check the correct question. 🎧27 SKIM

- ○ How can I learn how to roll my tongue?
- ○ Do you think tongue-rolling is a hereditary characteristic?
- ○ Can you roll your tongue?
- ○ How do you study the ability to roll the tongue?

Dr Hopper is a scientist that studies the ability of rolling the tongue in families.

2 Listen to Dr Hopper again and mark True or False. 🎧27 SCAN

	True	False
Scientists know why people can or can't roll their tongues.		
The results of the studies are inconclusive.		
Dr Hopper's sister can roll her tongue.		
If you practice, you can learn how to roll your tongue.		
Dr Hopper thinks the ability to roll the tongue is hereditary.		
The results of studies are similar: 65-80% of people in the world can't roll their tongues.		

YOUR TAKE

Who can roll their tongue in your family?
Do you think it is possible to learn how to roll the tongue?

Pronunciation Tongue twisters

A tongue twister is a sentence that is difficult to say because there's a lot of repetition of words and similar sounds.

1 Listen to the tongue twisters.

a She sells seashells by the seashore.

b How much wood could a woodchuck chuck if a woodchuck could chuck wood?

c Peter Piper picked a peck of pickled peppers.

2 Listen again and repeat.

3 I bet you can't say these tongue twisters very fast. Can you?

167

↑ Road to success

Body language
Quando aprendemos um idioma, geralmente concentramos nossos esforços na prática oral e escrita da língua e nos esquecemos de que nosso corpo também se comunica.
A linguagem corporal (gestos, postura, expressão facial e movimento dos olhos) é muito importante para quem aprende um novo idioma, porque ajuda a passar mensagens que ainda não sabemos comunicar com palavras.
Por isso, se você estiver em uma situação em que precise dizer alguma coisa em inglês mas ainda não saiba expressar isso corretamente, não tenha medo: use as palavras e a comunicação corporal. Essa combinação é sempre mais eficiente!

Unit 5 – Yes, we can!

Go to *Looking Back* on page 136 ▶ **87**

UNIT 6 Manners

ITINERARY

In this unit, you will develop the following competences:
- reading a handbook page to get general and specific information about good manners in public;
- learning expressions to talk about manners;
- reflecting on your words and attitudes to develop good communication manners;
- listening to subway announcements to get general and specific information about behavior in trains;
- reading about good manners in society to become a better citizen;
- using the imperative to make requests, give orders, or express rules;
- using expressions and the correct intonation to make polite requests;
- writing a note to say thank you.

Reading  A handbook

1 A handbook is a reference book that gives instructions. What do you know about handbooks? Complete the text. GENRE

| method | answer | information |

Handbooks can have .... about any topic. They are guides of information in a specific area or about a specific .... People read handbooks to find fast .... about something.

2 Read the book titles below. Which ones are handbooks?

3 Read a page from a handbook and answer: what title is more appropriate for this book? SKIM
- "How to Be a Respected Person"
- "Good Manners in Public"
- "A Guide to Libraries, Restaurants, and Parks"

Show Good Manners in Public!

Where do you go out in public? Public places you visit might include libraries, restaurants, and parks. Being in public often means being around lots of other people. Remember to treat them with respect. Showing respect lets others know that you care about them.

> **Different places require different manners. It is all right to shout and run at the park. But that would be bad manners at the library. Be aware of where you are and those around you!**

MARSICO, Katie. *Good manners in public*

Glossary

good manners: appropriate attitudes
bad manners: inappropriate attitudes
care: have affection
shout:

run:

4 Read again and choose the correct options. SCAN

  a When you are in libraries, restaurants, and parks, you are…
  - ◯ in public.
  - ◯ in private, alone.
  - ◯ around other people.

  b When you are around other people…
  - ◯ show that you care.
  - ◯ treat them with respect.
  - ◯ shout and run.

REFLECT
1. Why is it important to treat people with respect?
2. Why is it important to show people that you care about them?

Unit 6 – Manners

91

Vocabulary Manners

1 Classify these actions in the table on the next page. Then listen and check your work. 🎧29

Give up your seat to the elderly.

Cut in lines.

Litter.

Say "excuse me", "please", "I'm sorry", and "thank you".

Talk loud in movie theaters.

Cover your mouth when you sneeze or yawn.

Talk with your mouth full.

Turn your cell phone off in movie theaters.

Interrupt people when they are talking.

Hold your backpack in front of you on trains or buses.

92

GOOD MANNERS	BAD MANNERS
....	....

2 Complete the sentences with phrases from the table.

   a It's important to say .... because it makes people feel good.

   b I don't like when people .... because I want to listen to the movie, not the conversation.

   c When there are a lot of people in the train, you should hold .... so the passengers can walk in the corridor.

   d .... , but remember to wash your hands after that.

   e Don't .... ! Show that you respect other people in line.

3 Pair work. Complete these sentences with the phrases from the table and tell them to a partner.

   I always .... , and you?

   I don't .... , and I feel bad about it. What about you?

167

↑ Road to success

Communication manners

Independentemente do idioma, comunicar-se bem vai muito além das palavras que você escolhe; tem muito a ver com as suas atitudes.
As boas maneiras influenciam o modo como as pessoas veem você e como compreendem o que diz. Para demonstrá-las:
- não interrompa a conversa de outras pessoas;
- não termine as frases que alguém começou;
- pense antes de falar, para depois não se arrepender do que disse;
- olhe nos olhos da pessoa com quem estiver conversando;
- use **sempre** palavras educadas como "thank you", "please", "excuse me", "I'm sorry" etc.

Unit 6 – Manners

Listening Subway announcement

1 Subway announcements are voice messages for the subway passengers. What do you know about subway announcements? Write T (true) or F (false). **GENRE**

- ◯ Passengers can hear to subway announcements when they are at the station or on the trains.
- ◯ Subway announcements are recorded by famous people.
- ◯ The announcements can give station information, line information, warnings, or recommendations to the passengers.
- ◯ The subway announcements are often very long messages.

2 Listen to the subway announcements and order the pictures. 🎧30 **SKIM**

  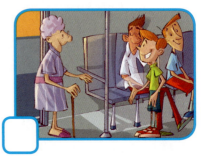

3 Listen again and answer. 🎧30 **SCAN**

a What color are the priority seats?
- ◯ Red.
- ◯ Green.

b Why do you hold your backpack in front of you?
- ◯ To give space to passengers who get on the train.
- ◯ To be near the doors.

c Where are the trash cans?
- ◯ In the trains.
- ◯ On the platforms.

In 2006, an MTA (Metropolitan Transportation Authority) spokesperson said that in the New York City subway, most of the warnings and recommendations are recorded by male voices and most of the information by female voices. He also said that it was a coincidence, but he believes that it was a good thing. He claims that psychologists believe people are more receptive to orders given by men and information given by women.

English · Crossroads · Citizenship

1 Read the text and match the sentences (1 to 4) to the images.

Good manners in society

Respecting other people and practicing good habits and simple attitudes are fundamental to have good social interactions in big cities.

On public transportation, respect the seats reserved for the elderly, the disabled, pregnant women, and parents with children ❶. Offer your seat to them on a crowded bus.

Respect the lines ❷ in banks and public services. Confusion creates problems that can extend for a long period.

Remember that there are other people with you on public transportation. When you listen to music on a bus, train, or the subway, use earphones ❸.

A correct attitude that is important to remember: throw your trash in the trash can. Trash on the streets causes floods ❹ which create traffic problems.

The good news is that a good action produces another good action. You only have to start.

Adapted from Brasil.gov.br

YOUR TAKE

1 Do people in your city practice these good manners?
2 What other examples of good manners can you name?

Grammar   Imperative

> **Imperative sentences** make requests, give orders, or express rules.

1 Read the signs with examples of the imperative. Mark **A** for an affirmative sentence or **N** for a negative sentence.

◯

◯

◯

◯

◯

2 Choose the correct alternative.
  a The imperative affirmative uses…
   ◯ the verb only.   ◯ the verb with *do*.
  b The imperative negative uses…
   ◯ the verb only.   ◯ the verb with *do not* (or *don't*).

3 Complete the sentences with the affirmative or negative form of the verbs in the box.

a .... the yellow line.

b .... your hands before you cook.

c .... the cake!

d .... your nose, dear!

e .... more fruits.

f .... , James! It's time to go to school!

Unit 6 – Manners

97

Speaking — Polite requests

We use the **imperative** to make simple requests. When we want to be more polite, we use "Could you...?" or "Would you please..." to make the request.

1 Listen and compare these two dialogs. Which one is more polite? 🎧31

Using imperatives	Using *would you...* and *could you...*
Delivery man: Mrs Goethals? **Mrs Goethals:** Yes? **Delivery man:** Sign here. **Mrs Goethals:** Give me your pen. **Delivery man:** Thanks. **Mrs Goethals:** Bye.	**Delivery man:** Mrs Goethals? **Mrs Goethals:** Yes? **Delivery man:** Could you sign here, please? **Mrs Goethals:** Sure. Would you please lend me your pen? **Delivery man:** Sure, no problem. Thanks. Have a nice day. **Mrs Goethals:** You too. Bye.

Pronunciation — Intonation in yes / no questions

1 In questions that we can answer with a *yes* or *no*, the intonation goes up in the end of the sentence. Listen and read. 🎧32

    Could you sign here, please?
    Would you please sign here?

2 Practice these dialogs with a partner. Use polite requests to make these interactions appropriate.

Flight attendant: Can I help you?
Girl: Give me an orange juice.
Flight attendant: OK. Is that all?
Girl: Bring some water for my mother.
Flight attendant: OK. Just a minute.

Teacher: The correct answer is 45.
Student: Repeat, teacher!
Teacher: 45.
Student: I don't understand. Explain again.
Teacher: OK. Let's review it.

Librarian: Can I help you?
Student: Get me the book *Oliver Twist*.
Librarian: Give me your library card.
Student: Thanks.
Librarian: Bye.

 A thank-you note

It is essential that you say "thank you" when someone does or says something nice to you. It is even more personal and thoughtful to write a thank-you note.

Preparing to write
1. Think about the person and the reason why you want to say thank you.

Draft
2. Write your note. Include your name, the person's name, the date, and the reason for the note. Some examples of reasons can be: a favor, a compliment, a present, advice, some help, etc. Example:

"Thank you for your help with the homework. You are great!"

3. Proofread your text.

Final version
4. Write the final version of your note on a card or nice paper. Give it to the person you want to say thank you to.

Proofreading TIP
Ask a classmate to proofread your text. Different eyes notice different things and can help a lot.

Go to *Looking Back* on page 136

Unit 6 – Manners

99

Stopover Units 5 & 6

1 Draw the faces according to the instructions.

a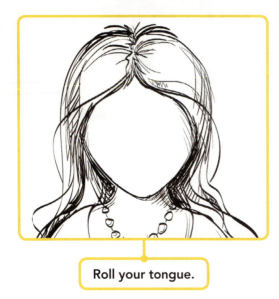
Roll your tongue.

b
Raise your right eyebrow.

c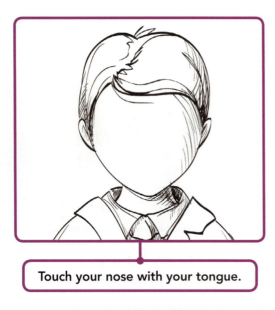
Touch your nose with your tongue.

d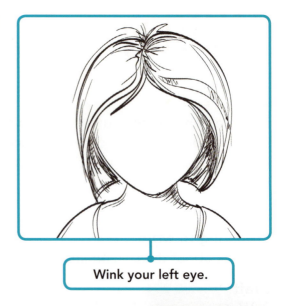
Wink your left eye.

2 This paragraph doesn't have spaces or punctuation. Can you separate the words and punctuate them correctly?

LISACANTSINGVERYWELLSHEHASSINGING
CLASSESTHREETIMESAWEEKSHEWANTS
TOHAVEAROCKBANDSOMEDAY

....
....
....

START

Instructions
1. Use a coin to move on the board.
2. Arrive first at the finish line and you're the winner.

HEADS = move 1 space

TAILS = move 2 spaces

1 You can't talk with your mouth full. Go back 2 spaces!

2 You never cut lines. Move 2 spaces.

4 You hold your backpack in front of you inside trains and buses. Move 2 spaces.

3 You litter parks and public areas! Go back 3 spaces!

5 You always give up your seat in trains and buses to women with babies. Move 3 spaces.

7 You and your friends talk loud in movie theaters! Go back 2 spaces!

6 You like to say "Excuse me", "Please", "I'm sorry", and "Thank you". Move 2 spaces.

Excuse me!

8 You never cover your mouth when you sneeze or yawn! Go back 1 space.

9 You don't turn your cell phone off in movie theaters! Go back 3 spaces!

FINISH

THE GOOD MANNERS GAME

Stopover

101

Extra Reading 3

1 What does a gentleman do and doesn't do, in your opinion?
2 Read and check if the text agrees with your opinion.

10 eternal truths of the gentlemanly life

By John Bridges

1. A gentleman says "please" and "thank you," readily and often.
2. A gentleman does not <u>disparage</u> the beliefs of others – whether they relate to matters of faith, politics, or sports teams.
3. A gentleman always carries a <u>handkerchief</u>, and is ready to lend it, especially to a <u>weeping</u> lady, should the need arise.
4. A gentleman never allows a door to <u>slam</u> in the face of another person – male or female, young or old, absolute stranger or longtime best friend.
5. A gentleman does not make jokes about race, religion, <u>gender</u>, or sexual orientation; neither does he find such jokes <u>amusing</u>.
6. A gentleman knows how to stand in line and how to wait his turn.
7. A gentleman is always ready to offer a <u>hearty</u> handshake.
8. A gentleman keeps his leather shoes <u>polished</u> and his fingernails clean.
9. A gentleman admits when he is wrong.
10. A gentleman does not <u>pick</u> a fight.

BRIDGES, John. *How to be a gentleman: a timely guide to timeless manners.*

Glossary

disparage: express a negative opinion about something

handkerchiefs:

weeping:

gender:

amusing: funny, entertaining
hearty: cordial, abundant
polished: brilliant, shiny
pick: provoke

3 Read again and match the photos to the sentences of the text.

3 Answer T (true) or F (false) according to the text.
- **a** ◯ A gentleman does not make jokes about gay people.
- **b** ◯ A gentleman thinks it is OK to laugh when a joke about religion is fun.
- **c** ◯ A gentleman doesn't have to wait in line.
- **d** ◯ A gentleman takes care of his personal hygiene.
- **e** ◯ A gentleman is nice to everybody, including people he doesn't know.

Extra Reading 3

103

Project 3

A handbook for new students

When people start learning a new language, they need much more than just grammar and vocabulary activities to become good students. They can also benefit a lot from other experienced learners who can share what they know. Students need strategies, suggestions, advice, inspiration, and motivation to keep going.

1 Feelings are very important when you are learning a language. When people start learning a new language, how do they feel?

 ◯ excited

 ◯ confused

 ◯ curious

 ◯ interested

 ◯ frustrated

 ◯ ....

2 Feeling confused and frustrated is not good, but these are common feelings when you start learning a language. How can you overcome those feelings? Use a dictionary to help you.

◯ Be persistent!   ◯ Have determination!

◯ Don't give up!   ◯ Don't panic! Keep calm.

◯ Relax for some time and go back to your studies later!

◯ Other: ....

3 Research!
Talk to your friends or family members who study English (or studied in the past). Ask them the following questions and take notes of their answers.

   a What suggestions or advice can you give to a new student of English?

   ....
   ....
   ....

b How do you stay motivated to study English?

....
....
....

4 Summarize your notes.
Use the information from activities 2, 3, and 4 and summarize your notes into the six best suggestions, advice, and motivational sentences. Use the dictionary, if necessary.

> **Remember!**
> - You learned many strategies on how to be a good language learner. What strategies are useful for you? Make notes.

1. ....
2. ....
3. ....
4. ....
5. ....
6. ....

5 Prepare a minibook to write your handbook. Use one sheet of regular-sized paper and follow the instructions below. Ask your teacher for help.

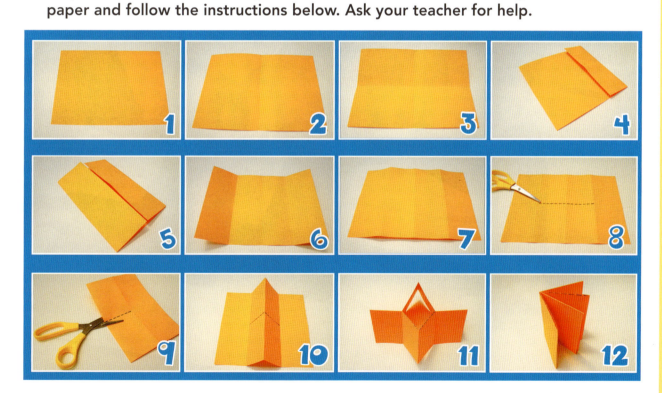

6 Prepare the cover and illustrate your handbook.

7 Share it with your classmates. Are the handbooks similar?

Project 3   105

UNIT 7 Hello?

ITINERARY

In this unit, you will develop the following competences:
- reading an instruction manual to learn how to make a call to Brazil;
- learning words and expressions to make and answer phone calls;
- listening to phone conversations to get general and specific information;
- learning language functions to have phone conversations;
- using the Present Continuous and the pronunciation of the contracted form of *to be* to talk about actions that are happening now;
- learning strategies to prepare for a conversation on the phone;
- reading about recycling to learn how to dispose of your old cell phone;
- writing instructions to use a cell phone.

107

Reading — Instruction manual

1 What do you know about instruction manuals? Choose the best options. **GENRE**

  a The person who reads a text of instructions wants to find answers to the question…
  - ○ "how do I do it?"
  - ○ "what's the name of…?"
  - ○ "how much does it cost?"

  b The language of a good text of instructions is…
  - ○ complex and detailed.
  - ○ objective and easy to understand.

  c In general, texts of instructions are…
  - ○ divided into many paragraphs.
  - ○ organized in topics.

2 Do you need instructions to make a phone call from a cell phone?

3 Read the text and answer the questions.

---

www.GoBrazil.about.com

Brazil Travel

Search

Making a collect call from a telephone in Brazil isn't difficult, but the recorded instructions are all in Portuguese.

Difficulty: Medium

1. To make a long distance call, you need the area code and a telephone company code (examples: Embratel – code 21, Telefonica – code 15).

2. Pick up the receiver and wait until you hear the dial tone.

3. To make a local collect call, dial 9090 and the telephone number.

4. To make a long distance collect call, dial 90, the telephone company code, the city code, and the telephone number. For example, to call Santos (area code 13) collect via Embratel, dial 90 - 21 - 13 + the telephone number in Santos.

5. After you dial a local or long distance collect call, you hear a message in Portuguese that says, "Collect Call. After the tone, say your name and the city you're calling from." The person on the other end hears a message that says, "Collect call — to accept it, stay on the line after identification." If the person accepts it, the phone call is completed and the conversation can start.

Adapted from GoBrazil.about.com

a Choose the best title for the text. SKIM
○ How to make a call from a telephone in Brazil.
○ How to make a collect call from a telephone.
○ How to make a collect call from a telephone in Brazil.

b Choose the best alternative to complete the sentences. SCAN

The instructions teach .... speakers to make phone calls in ....
The caller will hear a message in .... when the call is complete.

○ Portuguese – the USA – Portuguese
○ English – Brazil – Portuguese
○ English – Brazil – English

4 Match.

a Collect call
b Long distance call
c Pick up the receiver
d Dial
e Dial 9090 + telephone number
f Dial 90 + telephone company code + city code + telephone number
g "Collect Call. After the beep, say your name and the city you're calling from."
h "Collect call – to accept it, stay on the line after identification."

○ To make a long distance collect call.
○ The message people hear when they receive collect calls.
○ A telephone call to a different area code.
○ To make a local collect call.
○ The message you hear when you make a collect call.
○ A telephone call paid by the person receiving it.

5
Suppose you are in Palmas, Tocantins (area code: 63), and you are making a collect call to your friend who is in Palmas too. Your friend's telephone number is 5555 2014. What numbers do you dial? INFER

....

6
Now suppose you are in Natal, Rio Grande do Norte (area code: 84), and you are making a collect call to your friend in Belo Horizonte, Minas Gerais (area code: 31). Your friend's telephone number is 5555 7890. What numbers do you dial?

....
....

Unit 7 – Hello?

109

Vocabulary   Telephoning

1 Listen and read. 🎧 33

turn the phone on / off

answer the phone

leave a message

get the voice mail

make a call

hang up (end the call)

text

ring

2 Match the sentences.

a When you answer the phone, you say…

b If you have little time, do you prefer to make a call or…

c If you get the voice mail, do you prefer to end the call or…

d I turn on my cell phone in the morning and…

○ turn it off before I go to bed.

○ leave a message?

○ text?

○ "Hello?".

110

3 Complete the sentences with the words below:

> rings • make a call • texts • answer • leave a message • turn the phone off

a "Hi, I can't answer the phone now. Please, ... after the beep."
b Ms Jackson, could you excuse me? I need to ....
c If my phone .... when I'm in the shower, could you .... it, please?
d Mark, please end the call and .... The movie is about to start.
e She never calls her friends; she always ....

YOUR TAKE

1. How often do you call your friends?
2. How often do your friends call you?
3. Do you text your friends every day?
4. When you get the voice mail, do you leave a message or call back later?

Listening — Telephone conversations

1 Listen to the telephone conversations and order the pictures. 〔34〕 SKIM

2 Listen again and check the true sentences. 〔34〕 SCAN

Conversation 1
○ Denise studies at Jessica's school.

Conversation 2
○ Michael is the first to answer the phone.

Conversation 3
○ Amanda's mother answers the phone.

Conversation 4
○ Paulo's phone number is 555 9932.

Unit 7 – Hello?

111

Speaking Cell phone calls

1 Listen to these phone conversations. What's happening? 🎧35

Conversation 1

A: Hello?
B: Hello, Jessica?
A: Speaking
B: Hi, Jessica. This is Denise, from school.
A: Oh, hi Denise! How are you?
B: Fine, thanks. What are you doing now?
A: I'm not doing anything special.
B: Let's go to the mall!
A: Great, see you later! Bye!
B: Bye!

Conversation 2

A: Hello?
B: Hello, is Paulo there?
A: Paulo? There's nobody here by that name. I think you have the wrong number.
B: Is that 555-9832?
A: No, 555-9932.
B: Oh, I'm sorry.
A: That's OK.

2 Practice the dialogs with a partner. Use your real names!

Student A: Read the situations below.
Student B: Go to page 148.

> You are calling your friend to invite her / him to **go to the movies**. Your friend's number is 555 4637.

> You are calling to invite your friend to **study for the science test**. Your friend's number is 555 1318.

Student A: Now Student B calls you.

> Answer the phone and accept your friend's invitation.

> Answer the phone and say it's the **wrong number**. Your number is 555 4307.

112

Grammar Present Continuous

We use the Present Continuous to talk about an action that is happening now. Look at the position of the verb *to be*, the subject, and the main verb:

Interrogative → **Is she talking** to her mother?

Affirmative → No, **she is listening** to a voice message.

Interrogative → Who **are you talking** to?

Affirmative → **I'm not talking** to anybody. **I am listening** to my messages.

1 Complete the sentences with a word from the box.

affirmative • negative • interrogative

a We use subject + *to be* + not + verb -ing for the .... form.
b We use *to be* + subject + verb -ing for the .... form.
c We use subject + verb *to be* + verb -ing for the .... form.

2 Look at the photos and complete the questions / answers using the vocabulary in parentheses. Remember: you have to use the Present Continuous.

a

A: What is .... doing?
(text a message to a friend)
B: She is ....

b A: Is .... studying? (study / make a call)

B: No, she .... She is
....

Unit 7 – Hello?

113

c

A: What .... he doing? (use / public phone)

B: He is ....

d A: What .... they doing? (wait / phone call)

B: They are ....

e

A: What .... ? (take a message)

B: She is ....

f A: .... he ....? (work / sleep)

B: No, he .... He ....

g

A: What .... ? (walk)

B: ....

3 Answer.

a What are you doing now?

....

b Is your mother working now?

....

c What is your teacher doing now?

....

d Is your brother / sister sleeping now?

....

114

Pronunciation — Contractions – verb *to be*

1 Listen to the contracted forms of subject and verb *to be*. Then listen again and repeat. 🎧 36

I'm • You're • He's • She's • It's • We're • They're

2 Listen to the sentences and pay attention to the pronunciation of the verb *to be*. Then listen again and repeat. 🎧 37

a I'm studying.
b She's buying a cell phone.
c They're sleeping.
d I'm not doing anything.
e You're not working.

↑ Road to success

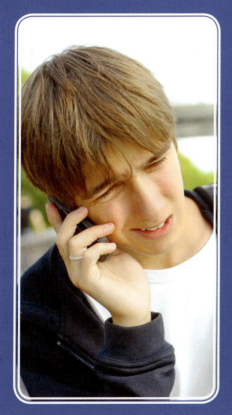

Telephoning strategies

Conversas ao telefone costumam ser mais difíceis de entender pelo fato de não haver contato visual entre os interlocutores ou linguagem corporal para ajudar na compreensão – depende-se apenas do som para saber o que a outra pessoa está querendo dizer.

Por isso, nessas situações é importante usar outras estratégias, como saber quais frases e vocabulários específicos costumam ser usados, qual é a sequência lógica que uma conversa deve seguir etc. Assim você conseguirá acompanhar melhor o que está sendo dito, porque saberá o que esperar da conversa.

Quando, por exemplo, ligamos para uma pessoa e ela não pode atender, a sequência lógica da conversa é:
- identificar-se (*This is…*);
- perguntar sobre a pessoa com a qual queremos conversar (*Can I speak to…?*);
- deixar recado (*Can I leave a message?*) ou não;
- agradecer e despedir-se (*Thank you. Goodbye*).

Unit 7 – Hello?

Geography — Crossroads — **English**

1 Do people in your house have cell phones? How many cell phones are there in your house? How often do the people in your house buy a new cell phone?

2 Are there old cell phones in your house that nobody uses anymore?

3 What can you do with your old cell phone?
- ◯ Sell.
- ◯ Put in the trash at home.
- ◯ Recycle.
- ◯ Donate.
- ◯ Discard properly.

4 Read the text and match the columns to form true sentences according to the text.

Three green ways to dispose of that old cell phone

Americans buy new cell phones every 18 months. With around 256 million cell phone users in the U.S., that's a lot of electronic waste. Cell phones contain a number of toxins that accumulate in the environment. These chemicals are associated with many types of health problems, like neurological disorders and cancer. That's the bad news. The good news is there are many free and easy ways to safely dispose of your old cell phone. Don't put your old phone in the trash. Check out a few ways you can use your old phone to do good or even make some money!

1. The Cell Phones For Soldiers organization accepts phones with or without the battery and gives them to U.S. troops around the world.
2. Charitable Recycling Program accepts donated cell phones and renovates them. These renovated phones are sent to communities around the world to provide safety and communication for people in need.
3. You can choose a charity in your community to benefit from your cell phone donation. The phones are renovated and distributed or recycled for money that the organization gives to the charity of your choice.

Adapted from EcoLocalizer.com

a Old cell phones are…
b Cell phones can't be put in the trash because they…
c The toxins in cell phones are bad for people because they…
d Some organizations receive donations of old cell phones and…

- ◯ renovate them to give to people who need them.
- ◯ electronic waste.
- ◯ can cause neurological disorders and cancer.
- ◯ pollute the environment with toxins.

Writing: Instructions to use a cell phone

Your brother / sister is borrowing your cell phone for a week. Write him / her instructions to **make a call** and **text a message** on your cell phone.

Preparing to write

1. (Use your cell phone. If you don't have a cell phone, ask your mother / father to lend you one.) Go to "settings" and change the language of your cell phone to "English". That way, all the buttons and commands are in English.
2. Turn off your cell phone and turn it on again, paying attention to all the buttons and commands you click to make a call and text a message. Make notes of the English names of the buttons and commands.
3. Read the characteristics of an instructional text again on page 108.

Draft

4. Write the instructions to make a call. If necessary, use a dictionary.
5. Write the instructions to text a message.
6. Proofread your text.

Final version

7. Write all the instructions in steps and include a title.

Share

8. Hand in your instructions to a classmate and ask him / her to test if your text is clear and correct. (If they can make a call and text a message using your instructions, it means your text is clear and correct!)

The word telephone has its origins in the Greek words *téle*, "far," and *phone*, "voice, sound." There are controversies about who invented the device. Although the Scotsman Alexander Graham Bell has become famous for the invention, it is believed that the Italian Antonio Meucci was the first person to be able to assemble the device, around 1860. The first cell phones were developed much later, in 1956. However, they were not practical since they weighed about 40 kilos!

Go to *Looking Back* on page 137

UNIT 8
Art is everywhere

ITINERARY

In this unit, you will develop the following competences:
- reading an interview to learn more about the life of a graffiti artist;
- learning words to talk about artists and forms of art;
- listening to a dialog in an art gallery to get general and specific information about an exhibition;
- reading about graffiti to create your own signature;
- writing a label to identify your graffiti signature;
- learning how to use emphasis to express your opinion about art;
- learning expressions to give a positive or negative opinion about art;
- contrasting the use of Yes / No questions vs. Wh-questions to ask and answer about art.

Reading — Interview with a graffiti artist

1 How much do you know about interviews? Circle the correct answer. **GENRE**

An interview is a *text / conversation* between two (or more) people where the interviewer asks questions to obtain information from the interviewee(s). They can be published or broadcast on TV and radio. There are many kinds of interviews and they can vary from very *formal / informal* (similar to conversations) to more closed (with options of fixed responses). When they are *published / broadcast*, you usually read the question and the answer. The names of the interviewer and the interviewee usually appear in the first questions and, for the following questions, we read only their *nicknames / initials*. Some interviews are also part of surveys and can be conducted by companies that collect public *opinion / names*.

2 Read the interview and answer the questions.

I'M A GRAFFITI ARTIST

12-year-old Solveig Barlow, from Brighton, England, is the new sensation in the graffiti world. She talks about her short, but amazing career.

BBC: Tell us about your first graffiti work.

Solveig Barlow: At first I was a bit scared of the size of the wall and trying to cover it all but as soon as I got going it was the last thing on my mind. My second painting was really big and it wasn't any harder to do than the first one.

BBC: Where do you do graffiti?

SB: I do my graffiti on walls I'm allowed to draw on. It's not a good idea to do it anywhere, 'cause that's illegal.

BBC: What is your work process?

SB: When I make a piece, I design it first in my sketchbook before I go to the wall.

BBC: What do you like to paint?

SB: I really love to make scenes or pictures with characters as I think it makes them more interesting.

120

BBC: Where does your inspiration come from?

SB: My inspiration comes from a lot of different places. I try to make every painting different from the last.

BBC: What do adults think of your work?

SB: I like the response I get from adults when they see my work. Many of them think I get help but when they watch me painting they can see that's not what happens.

BBC: What are your plans for the future?

SB: Sometimes I wonder if I will still do graffiti when I am older. I like to think I will because I love drawing and stuff. But if not, perhaps I'll be doing something else exciting."

Adapted from News.BBC.co.uk

Glossary

amazing: incredible
scared: in panic
allowed: permitted
draw: make a picture with lines or traces
sketchbook: a notebook used for drawing

a How old is Solveig Barlow?

....

b Where is she from?

....

c Does she draw on any wall she wants?

....

d Does she want to work with graffiti in the future?

....

3 Answer T (true) or F (false).

  a Solveig doesn't think about drawing before she goes to the wall. ◯
  b She thinks the use of characters makes the scenes more interesting. ◯
  c She tries to make her paintings similar to each other. ◯
  d Adults believe somebody helps her with the drawings. ◯

Unit 8 – Art is everywhere

121

Vocabulary Arts

Art	Artist
painting	painter
sculpture	sculptor
architecture	architect
music	musician
poetry	poet
drama	actors / actresses
dance	dancers
graffiti	graffiti artist
photography	photographer
illustration	illustrator

1 Complete the sentences with the correct words. Then listen and check your work. 🎧38

Solveig Barlow is a <u>graffiti artist</u>. You can see her <u>graffiti works</u> in Brighton, Essex, England.

a A professional .... creates a visual representation for a text or subject. You can see .... in many types of media, including books, magazines, comic books, and even newspapers.

b A professional .... can perform many types of ....: modern, jazz, tap, ethnic, classical ballet, or dances created by a choreographer.

c Wedding .... is a very popular area for a .... to work. They can also work for newspapers or taking pictures of models and products.

d .... is a very old art; it probably originated in Ancient Greece. A professional .... performs in theaters, movies, TV shows, or advertisements.

e Mario Quintana is a Brazilian ...., famous for talking about simple things in his texts. "Poeminha do Contra" is an example of the simplicity of his ....

f An .... designs and constructs buildings. The city of Brasilia is an example of modern ....

2 Can you name...

a a famous sculptor?
....

b a classical musician?
....

c a Spanish painter?
....

3 What's your favorite art form? Who is your favorite artist?
....
....
....

122

Listening An exhibition

1 Listen and answer: what kind of exhibition are they visiting? 🎧39 SKIM

2 Listen again and check the correct information. 🎧39 SCAN

RICHARD BAXTER (b.1968)
Woman on the street, 1997
Black and white photograph
Collection of Trevor Reinhold

RICHARD BAXTER (b.1968)
Woman on the street, 1997
Oil on canvas
Collection of Trevor Reinhold

RICHARD BAXTER (b.1997)
Woman on the street, 1968
Black and white photograph
Collection of Trevor Reinhold

YOUR TAKE

1. Do you visit art exhibitions?
   ....
   ....

2. What kind of art exhibition do you like to visit?
   ....
   ....

Unit 8 – Art is everywhere

123

English | Crossroads | Arts

Graffiti

Graffiti is not a modern expression. Greeks, Romans, Egyptians, Mayans, and Vikings practiced some kind of graffiti art in their cultures.

The modern version of graffiti appeared in the end of the 1960s in Paris, and in the 1970s it gained popularity in the United States (New York and Philadelphia) and other parts of the world, including Brazil (São Paulo).

Graffiti is an element of pop culture and it usually communicates a social message but when it is displayed in non authorized public places, it is illegal and considered an act of vandalism.

Styles of graffiti writing

Graffiti writing is the act of writing letters with graffiti style. There are many styles of writing, fonts, and letters in the art of graffiti:

Tag

A *tag* is a stylized signature of the artist, in a single solid color.

Throwie

A *throwie* is usually a signature with one color for the outline and another color for the fill.

Piece

A *piece* is a large graffiti painting that displays 3-D effects, arrows, color-transitions, and other artistic effects.

Adapted from HowToDrawGraffiti.net

YOUR TAKE

1. Answer.
   a Is graffiti cool? Is it annoying? Is it a crime? Justify your answer.
   ....
   ....
   ....

   b When does graffiti make the city more beautiful? More visually polluted?
   ....
   ....
   ....

   c Is it right to spray graffiti on a private property without permission?
   ....
   ....
   ....

   d In which situations would you give permission for someone to spray graffiti on your property?
   ....
   ....
   ....

   e What is the best punishment for graffiti artists who don't respect private property?
   ◯ They have to clean it.
   ◯ They have to go to prison.
   ◯ They have to pay a financial compensation.

1 **Follow the steps to create your individualized and personalized graffiti signature.**

> 1. Define the content of your signature: is it your complete name, the last name, or a nickname?
> 2. Define the style of your signature: tag, throwie, or piece.
> 3. Choose a font style.
> 4. Play with the letters, style, and colors before you draw the final version. Experiment with different sizes, color combinations, and symbols.
> 5. When you are happy with your signature, draw the final version on a sheet of paper.

BY THE WAY... Did you know that National Graffiti Day is celebrated on March 27, the date when Ethiopian Alex Vallauri (1949-1987) died? Vallauri is considered one of the graffiti pioneers in Brazil.

Adapted from Educacao.UOL.com.br

125

Writing — Identification label for your graffiti signature

A label is the text that accompanies an object and gives basic information about it. Your class is organizing an **exhibit** of all the students graffiti signatures. Write an identification label for your signature.

Preparing to write
1. Choose the information you want to give. Identification labels usually bring the name of the artist, the title of the work, place where the work was made, date, the technique used, the size (when available), the current owner or copyright holder of the image, and how the museum got the object. Example:

Vallauri, Alex (name of the artist)
Roasted chicken queen,
New York (USA) (title of the work, place where the work was made)
1983 (date)
stencil paint on wall (technique)
Unknown copyright holder of the image

Draft
2. Write the information in the form of a list of items on a piece of paper.
3. Think about the size of your label considering the information you want to give.
4. Cut a piece of paper in the appropriate size to write all the information.
5. Proofread your text.

Final version
6. Write all the information in the label. The information has to be clean and easy to read.

Share
7. Put your label next to your signature, in a place where people can read it.
8. The class decides on a date for the exhibition opening and invites other classes, school staff, family, and friends.

↑ Road to success

Arts help memorization

Com um pouco de criatividade e usando representações artísticas de seus significados, é possível memorizar os significados das palavras. Por exemplo:

L👀K

Note que as letras "o" de **look** foram transformadas em olhos, o que ajuda a memorizar o significado da palavra: look = 'olhar'.

Veja outro exemplo:

GROWING

A palavra **growing** significa 'crescendo', e é exatamente isso o que as letras estão fazendo. Observe mais este exemplo:

FALL

As letras da palavra **fall** ('cair') dão a ideia de queda. Que tal usar a imaginação e criar representações para estas palavras?

spray – polluted – prison

Pronunciation — Emphasis

We pronounce some words with more stress or prolonged sound when we want to emphasize them. Sometimes the word that is emphasized gives a different meaning or intention to the sentence. This kind of emphasis can be used to express your opinion about works of art.

1 Listen and read. 🎧 40

I **really** like it. (You **love** it.)   I don't like it **at all**. (You **hate** it.)

2 Read these sentences and emphasize the words in bold. Then match the sentences to their meanings.

a In **my** opinion, this painting is really interesting.

b In my opinion, **this** painting is really interesting.

c In my opinion, this painting is **really** interesting.

○ This painting is interesting, not that painting.

○ This is my opinion, not your opinion.

○ I think the painting is very interesting.

Speaking — Opinions

1 Listen to the two friends talking about the painting. 🎧 41

Emma: How do you like it?
Ben: In my opinion, it's horrible.
Emma: I like it. I think it's interesting.

ask for opinion:	Other expressions to…	
	give an opinion:	
	Positive:	Negative:
What do you think about it?	In my opinion, it's cool.	In my opinion, it's awful.
What is your opinion about it?	I think it's genius.	I don't think it's interesting.
	I really like it.	I don't like it all.

2 Talk to a partner about the following pieces of art.

Unit 8 – Art is everywhere

127

Grammar Yes / no questions × wh-questions

A: Is she studying?
B: Yes, she is.
A: What is she studying?
B: She's studying painting.

A: Does he have guitar classes?
B: Yes, he does.
A: When does he have guitar classes?
B: He has guitar classes on Fridays.

1 Read the dialogs above and answer: what's the difference between the first and the second questions in each dialog?

....
....

2 Look at the picture. Then match the questions to the answers.

a Is he a musician?
b Where does he play?
c When does he play there?
d What does he play?
e Does he play other instruments?
f Is he playing now?
g What is he playing now?

○ He plays on the streets.
○ He plays on the streets from Friday to Sunday.
○ He plays the guitar.
○ Yes, he does. Piano, drums, saxophone...
○ Yes, he is playing on the corner.
○ He is playing a famous folk song.
○ Yes, he is.

128

3 **Complete the questions appropriately.**

A: **Is he** studying for the test?
B: Yes, he is.
A: **Who is he** studying with?
B: He is studying with a classmate.

a A: .... building their sculptures?
B: They are building their sculptures in the park.
A: .... participating in a competition?
B: No, they aren't.

b A: .... go to the dance school?
B: She goes to the dance school by subway.
A: .... take the red line?
B: Yes, she does.

c A: .... take photographs of people?
B: No, they don't.
A: .... photograph?
B: They photograph nature.

Go to *Looking Back* on page 137

Stopover Units 7 & 8

1 Find the illustrations according to the clues below.

- He is driving a car.
- He is singing.
- He is speaking on the phone.
- He is reading the newspaper.
- He is sleeping, but he is not sleeping at home.
- He isn't playing the piano, but he is playing a musical instrument.
- He isn't eating at home. He is at a restaurant.
- Is he watching TV? Yes, he is.

130 Units 7 & 8

Optical illusions

1 Do you see white or black dots?

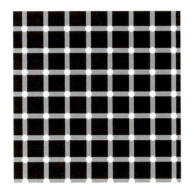

- **a** ◯ White, but I see black dots when I move my eyes.
- **b** ◯ Black, but I see white dots when I move my eyes.
- **c** ◯ There are no dots.

2 Are these lines parallel or not?

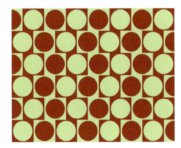

◯ No.   ◯ Yes.

3 Are these circles moving to the right or to the left?

◯ They are moving to the right.
◯ Both. It depends on where you look.

4 What do you see: a young woman or an old one?

◯ Young.   ◯ Old.   ◯ Both.

5 Do these man have different heights?

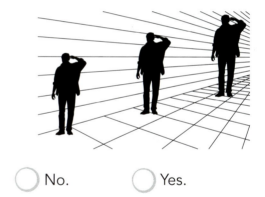

◯ No.   ◯ Yes.

6 What do you see here?

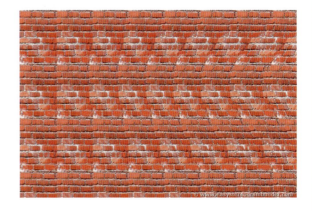

....

Stopover   131

Extra Reading 4

1 Read these dialogs on the phone and answer the questions.

Mystery Stories

By David Helwig

'Hello.'
'Is he there?'
'Who is it you want?'
'Oh for Christ's sake. Emmanuel. Would you just put him on?'
'I'm afraid you've got the wrong number.'
'Is that 721-8543?'
'Yes.'
'Then where is he?'
'This is my number. I just moved in here, and it's the number they gave me. Your friend must have moved or changed his number.'
'So what's his new number?'
'I don't know. I don't know anything about him. This is my number, and that's all I can tell you.'
'You don't have his new number.'
'No.'
'Well, has he moved?'
'I don't have any idea. I don't know the man, and I don't know his number, and I'm going to hang up now.'
***
'Yes, hello, could I speak to Mr Emmanuel, please?'
'I'm sorry, but there's no such person at this number.'
'Excuse me?'
'He's not here.'
'Please, when will he be available?'
'You have the wrong number.'
'But I was told…'
'I'm sorry, but he's not here.'
'He will be back?'
'No.'
'He will not be back.'
'He doesn't live here.'
'He is living where?'
'I don't know.'
'It is important for me to speak with Mr Emmanuel.'

'Look. This is my number. I just had a new telephone put in, and this is the number they gave me. I don't know anything about the man you're looking for. He must have changed his number or gone away.'
'Mr Emmanuel has gone away?'
'I don't know.'
'Where has he gone?'
'I don't know.'
'You don't know where he has gone?'
'Right.'
'It is important.'
'I'm sure it is. But I can't help you.'

Available at: Books.google.com

a Who is Emmanuel?
- ◯ The person who answers the phone calls.
- ◯ The person the callers want to talk to.

b Is it the right telephone number?

....
....
....

c Does the person that answers the phone calls know Emmanuel?

....

2 Read the dialogs again and find...

a a sentence similar to "Who do you want to speak to?"

....
....

b a sentence similar to "Let me talk to him, please."

....
....

c a sentence similar to "This is the end of the conversation."

....
....

d a sentence similar to "There's nobody here by that name."

....
....

e a sentence similar to "I'd like to talk to Emmanuel."

....
....

Extra Reading 4

Project 4

A tribute to an artist in stencil

 A tribute is something that you do, say, or build to show that you respect and admire someone.

 Stencil uses paper, cardboard, or a sheet of hard plastic to create an image or text that is reproducible. The image is cut out and then transferred to a surface using paint.

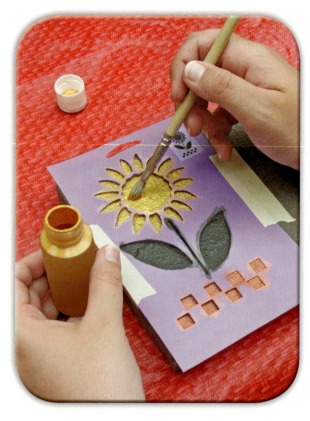

1 Name a contemporary artist you admire. Why do you admire him / her?
....
....

2 What do you know about this artist?
....
....

3 What don't you know about him / her? Make a list of five questions about the things you don't know but you want to find out.

Where does she live?
What does she do in her free time?
Is she married?

1. ....
2. ....
3. ....
4. ....
5. ....

Units 7 & 8

4 Research!
Use the school library or the Internet to find the answers to your questions in activity 3.

5 Think about an image you associate with the artist. For example, for Rihanna you can choose an **umbrella** (name of one of her hit songs).

6 Draw or print the image on paper. Use a hard type of paper for better results (for example, acetate, poster board, etc). This image must be in black and white.

7 Cut out the image using a cutter knife.

8 Transfer your stencil to another surface: a poster, your notebook, etc. Use your creativity: add colors, create a background, etc.

9 Present your tribute to the class. Use the information from activities 1, 2, and 3.

"This is my tribute to an artist I admire: Rihanna. I admire her because she is a very talented singer and dancer. She is from Barbados but she lives in the USA and…"

Project 4

Looking Back at UNIT 5

Now I can...			Learn more about it:
read a chart about tongue rolling.			
talk about body tricks.			Find out more about our body in *101 things you didn't know about your body*, by John Townsend.
use *can* and possessive adjectives.			Study the information on page 144 in the *Grammar Reference* section.
calculate percentages.			
write a chart to illustrate the results of a survey.			Write a chart of your own at <http://nces.ed.gov/nceskids/creategraph/default.aspx>.
challenge my friends and respond.			
listen to an explanation about tongue rolling.			
practice tongue twisters.			Look at other examples of tongue twisters (with audio) at <http://learnenglishkids.britishcouncil.org/en/tongue-twisters>.
use my body to communicate.			

Looking Back at UNIT 6

Now I can...			Learn more about it:
read a handbook page about good manners in public.			Read the guide *Good manners in public*, by Katie Marsico.
talk about manners.			
develop good communication manners.			
listen to subway announcements about behavior in trains.			Go to <http://soundcloud.com> and search *subway announcements* to listen to more subway announcements.
read about good manners in society to become a better citizen.			Learn more about etiquette and good manners reading the book *How rude!: the teenagers' guide to good manners, proper behavior, and not grossing people out*, by Alex J. Packer.
use the imperative to make requests, give orders, or express rules.			Study the information on page 145 in the *Grammar Reference* section.
make polite requests.			
write a thank-you note.			

136   Looking Back

Looking Back at UNIT 7

Now I can...	😊 😟	Learn more about it:
read an instruction manual to learn how to make a call to Brazil.		
make and answer phone calls.		Want to know more about how cell phones work? Read *Cell phone science: what happens when you call and why*, by Michele Sequeira and Michael Westphal.
listen to phone conversations.		
use the Present Continuous.		Study the information on page 146 in the *Grammar Reference* section.
read about recycling to learn how to dispose of your old cell phone.		At <http://www.e-lixo.org> you can find more information on how to properly discard electronic devices. There's also a map displaying places close to your home that process this type of waste.
write instructions to use a cell phone.		
prepare for a conversation on the phone.		

Looking Back at UNIT 8

Now I can...	😊 😟	Learn more about it:
read an interview about the life of a graffiti artist.		Watch the documentary *Aerosol* (2004, Spain) and see how interviews were used to create the film.
talk about forms of art and artists.		
listen to a dialog in an art gallery about an exhibition.		
read about graffiti to create my own signature.		Read the story of Nick, the graffiti artist, in the book *Graffiti*, by Lynne Lambright.
write a label to identify my graffiti signature.		Visit a virtual museum at <http://www.museevirtuel-virtualmuseum.ca> and pay attention to how art work is labeled.
use emphasis to express my opinion.		
give a positive or negative opinion about art.		
contrast the use of yes / no questions vs. wh-questions.		Study the information on page 147 in the *Grammar Reference* section.

Looking Back

137

Review Units 5 to 8

1 Read the chart below. Then write three affirmative sentences and three negative ones about what they **can** or **can't** do.

✔ = yes
✘ = no

	Karina	Marcelo	Vera
whistle	✔	✔	✔
dance	✔	✔	✘
do tongue tricks	✘	✔	✘
cook	✘	✘	✔
speak Spanish	✔	✘	✔

Karina can whistle.
Karina and Vera can't do tongue tricks.

a ....
b ....
c ....
d ....
e ....
f ....

2 Write sentences about the signs below.

 Don't bring food.

 Respect the kangaroos.

a ....

b ....

c ....

d ....

3 Answer the questions about the pictures. Use complete sentences.

a Are they dancing?

b What are they doing?

c Is he sleeping?

d Is she talking on the phone?

e What is she doing?

f Are you studying English?

Review

Grammar Reference

Unit 1

Simple Present – affirmative / negative

AFFIRMATIVE

SUBJECT	VERB	COMPLEMENT
I You We They	go	to school in the morning.

NEGATIVE

SUBJECT	AUXILIAR VERB	VERB	COMPLEMENT
I You We They	don't	go	to school in the morning.

1 Choose a verb from the box and complete these sentences with the **affirmative** or **negative** form.

live • speak • play • go • have • like

a We .... to talk on the phone for hours.
b They .... Spanish very well.
c I .... many books at home.
d You .... in an apartment near the school.
e We .... to study on Sundays.
f You .... many friends at school.
g Many students .... musical instruments in my class.
h My brother and I .... to bed at 11 pm.

2 Read the instructions and write sentences about you.
A type of food that you don't like.
I don't like Japanese food.

a A TV show you watch every day.
....

b A school subject that you don't like.
....

c The street where you live.
....

d The days when you don't go to school.
....

e The games that you like to play.
....

Unit 2

Simple Present – affirmative / negative

AFFIRMATIVE		
SUBJECT	VERB	COMPLEMENT
He She It	goes	to school in the morning.

NEGATIVE			
SUBJECT	AUXILIAR VERB	VERB	COMPLEMENT
He She It	doesn't	go	to school in the morning.

> **Attention!**
> Verbs ending in -o, -ch, -sh, -x, and -z add -es.
> **Maria goes** to an American school.
> **She watches** lucha libre on TV.
>
> Verbs ending in **consonant** + -y drop the -y and add -ies:
> **Sherap studies** every day at the monastery.
>
> The verb have is **irregular**:
> **He has** a lot of homework to do.
>
> For the other verbs, we add **-s**.
> **She plays** the guitar so well!
> **He works** in the hospital.
> **Marcus speaks** German and Russian.

1 Write sentences about Ryan using the Simple Present.

Ryan Scott Phillips Age:12

2 What about you? Write some sentences about the things you do during the day.
I have breakfast at 7:30 am.

Grammar Reference 141

Unit 3

Simple Present – interrogative (yes / no questions) and short answers

AUXILIAR VERB	SUBJECT	VERB	COMPLEMENT
Do	I / you / we / they	live	in a house?
Does	he / she / it		

AFFIRMATIVE SHORT ANSWERS

Yes,	I / you / we / they	do.
	he / she / it	does.

NEGATIVE SHORT ANSWERS

No,	I / you / we / they	don't.
	he / she / it	doesn't.

1 Complete these questions.

(he / live)
A: <u>Does he live</u> with his grandmother?
B: Yes, <u>he does</u>. Her name is Olga.

a (you / speak)
A: .... other languages?
B: No, ... I speak Portuguese only.

b (she / go)
A: .... to school by bus?
B: ...., she .... She takes the bus at 6:30 am.

c (they / have)
A: .... lunch at home?
B: .... They have lunch at school.

d (it / have)
A: This math problem is impossible! .... a solution?
B: .... It's on your book.

2 Complete this dialog with questions.

A: Let's have some pizza!
B: Great! Wait... .... pepperoni? (have)
A: Yes, ...
What's the problem?
B: I don't like pepperoni!
A: Do you want to order another pizza?
B: No, that's OK. .... ketchup? (have)
A: Ketchup? With pizza?
B: Yes, why not?
A: I prefer olive oil. .... some olive oil? (want)
B: Oh, yes, please. And... .... mustard with your pizza?
A: Mustard? Eww!

142   Grammar Reference

Unit 4
Adverbs

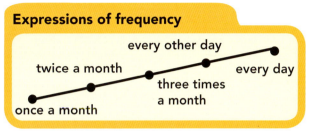

I **always** drink water in the morning. (I drink water *every day*.)
I **often (frequently)** walk to school. (I walk to school *three times a week*.)
I **sometimes** play video games. (I play video games *every other day / twice a week*.)
I **rarely** visit my uncle Tom. (I visit my uncle Tom *once a year*.)
I **never** do homework on Sundays.

Adverbs of frequency come **before** the verb.
Expressions of frequency come **after** the verb.

1 Look at this chart with Anne's activities and answer the questions.

ACTIVITY	MON	TUE	WED	THU	FRI	SAT	SUN
have piano lessons			✓				✓
have computer classes							
go to a library					✓		
ride a bicycle			✓		✓		
eat salad		✓	✓	✓	✓	✓	✓

a How often does she have piano lessons?
....
....

b How often does she have computer classes?
....
....

c How often does she go to a library?
....
....

d How often does she ride a bicycle?
....
....

e How often does she eat salad?
....
....

2 What about you? Answer these questions.
a How often do you help your mother at home?
....

b How often do you sleep in the afternoon?
....

c How often do you cook?
....

d How often do you play on the street?
....

Grammar Reference

Unit 5

Can

We use *can* to talk about **abilities**.

CAN	SUBJECT	VERB	COMPLEMENT
Can	I / you / he / she / it / we / they	sing	an English song?

AFFIRMATIVE SHORT ANSWERS			NEGATIVE SHORT ANSWERS		
Yes,	I / you / he / she / it / we / they	can.	No,	I / you / he / she / it / we / they	can't.

1 Complete these questions and answers.

a A: .... write with your left hand?
B: Yes, ... But I can't read what I write...

b A: Can she play soccer with the boys?
B: .... She is a very good player.

c A: .... come to my party next Saturday?
B: No, they can't. They have a family dinner.

d A: The test can't be tomorrow. .... be next Wednesday?
B: No. On Wednesday there is a history test.

e A: Can he teach Spanish?
B: .... His parents are from Chile.

Possessive adjectives

They are used to indicate possession.

I live with **my** family.
You live with **your** family.
He lives with **his** family.
She lives with **her** family.
It lives with **its** family.

We live with **our** families.
You live with **your** families.
They live with **their** families.

2 Complete these sentences with a possessive adjective.

a We have a new teacher in .... school.
b The school has a new layout in .... homepage on the Internet.
c She likes to dance, but .... movements are not very elegant.
d I don't see .... brother very often because he lives in another city.
e You and your family respect .... traditions from Italy.
f You never listen to .... mother's advice!
g They don't like .... new school uniforms.
h Leo eats .... hamburgers without mustard or ketchup.

Grammar Reference

Unit 6

Imperative

We use the imperative to make requests, give orders, or express rules.

AFFIRMATIVE
Open the door.
Close your books.
Repeat after me.
Eat your vegetables.

NEGATIVE
Don't close the window.
Don't enter.
Don't talk in the library.
Don't use this bathroom.

1 Complete the sentences with the affirmative or negative form of the verbs in the box.

touch • wash • eat • walk • read • copy

a .... special shampoo to wash your dog.

b Dad, ... the cookies! You are on a diet!

c .... the instructions for me, please.

d Hey! .... the answers from your friend!

e Michael, ... the walls! The paint is still fresh!

f .... on the grass!

Grammar Reference 145

Unit 7

Present Continuous

We use the Present Continuous to talk about an action that is happening now.

AFFIRMATIVE

SUBJECT	VERB TO BE	VERB (-ING)	COMPLEMENT
I	am		
You	are		
He	is		
She	is	waiting	for an answer.
It	is		
We	are		
They	are		

NEGATIVE

SUBJECT	VERB TO BE + NOT	VERB (-ING)	COMPLEMENT
I	am not		
You	are not		
He	is not		
She	is not	waiting	for an answer.
It	is not		
We	are not		
They	are not		

INTERROGATIVE

VERB TO BE	SUBJECT	VERB (-ING)	COMPLEMENT
Am	I		
Are	you		
Is	he		
Is	she	waiting	for an answer?
Is	it		
Are	we		
Are	they		

1 Look at the photos and write questions or sentences using the vocabulary in parentheses.

a A: What are they doing? (to have breakfast)
B: ....
....

b A: What is he doing? (to wink)
B: ....
....

c  A: What is she doing? (to cook)
B: ....
....

d A: What are you doing? (to wash hands)
B: ....
....

e  A: Are they watching a movie? (to watch a concert)
B: No, they ....
....
They are ....
....

f A: Is she talking on the phone? (to text / dial)
B: No, she ....
....
She ....
....

146 Grammar Reference

Unit 8

Simple Present

QUESTION WORD	AUXILIARY VERB	SUBJECT	COMPLEMENT
What	do	you	like to eat?
Who	do	you	know in my class?
Where	does	Steve	live?
When	do	you	have English classes?
How	does	she	go to school?

Present Continuous

QUESTION WORD	TO BE	SUBJECT	VERB (-ING)	COMPLEMENT
What	is	she	doing	now?
Where	are	they	going	to have lunch?
When	is	Laura	playing	volleyball?
How	are	you	studying	for the test?

Note:
Who is talking to you?
(*Who* is the question word and the subject of the sentence.)

1 Write appropriate questions for each answer.

a
A: ....
....
at home? (to help)
B: Yes, he does.

b A: ....
....
for the doctor? (to wait)
B: Yes, she is.

c
A: ....
....
(to do)
B: They are picking apples.

d A: ....
....
(to work)
B: They work at a flower shop.

e
A: ....
....
(to play)
B: She plays the violin.

f A: ....
....
(to kiss)
B: She is kissing her grandfather.

Grammar Reference

UNIT 7 Page 112

1 Listen to these phone conversations. What's happening? [35]

Conversation 1

A: Hello?
B: Hello, Jessica?
A: Speaking
B: Hi, Jessica. This is Denise, from school.
A: Oh, hi Denise! How are you?
B: Fine, thanks. What are you doing now?
A: I'm not doing anything special.
B: Let's go to the mall!
A: Great, see you later! Bye!
B: Bye!

Conversation 2

A: Hello?
B: Hello, is Paulo there?
A: Paulo? There's nobody here by that name. I think you have the wrong number.
B: Is that 555-9832?
A: No, 555-9932.
B: Oh, I'm sorry.
A: That's OK.

2 Now practice the dialogs with a partner. Use your real names!

Student B: Student A calls you.

Answer the phone and say it's the **wrong number**. Your number is 555 4673.

Answer the phone and accept your friend's invitation.

Student B: Now you call Student A.

You are calling to invite your friend to **play video game**. Your friend's number is 555 0051.

You are calling to invite your friend to **go to the park**. Your friend's number is 555 4407.

148   A ⇄ B

Minidictionary

English-Portuguese

More than 700 entries!

WITH STAR RATING

> **adj.** = adjective
> **adv.** = adverb
> **conj.** = conjunction
> **deter.** = determiner
> **interj.** = interjection
> **mod. v.** = modal verb
> **n.** = noun
> **numb.** = number
> **prep.** = preposition
> **pron.** = pronoun
> **v.** = verb

All red words have a "star rating":
★★★ The most common and basic English words
★★ Very common words
★ Fairly common words

A

ability /əˈbɪləti/ n. ★★★ habilidade *He has the ability to roll his tongue.*

about /əˈbaʊt/ adv. prep. ★★★ sobre *I like to talk about films.*

above /əˈbʌv/ adv. ★★★ acima *The roof is above the house.*

accept /əkˈsept/ v. ★★★ aceitar *They accept cash and cards in this store.*

accommodation /əˌkɑməˈdeɪʃ(ə)n/ noun ★★ acomodação, alojamento *When we camp, we stay in students' accommodations.*

according to /əˈkɔrdɪŋ ˌtu/ prep. ★★ de acordo com *According to the teacher, this exercise is easy.*

add /æd/ v. ★★★ adicionar *Add me as a friend in this social network.*

advantage /ədˈvæntɪdʒ/ n. ★★★ vantagem *Being kind to people has more advantages than you think.*

advertise /ˈædvərˌtaɪz/ v. ★★ anunciar *They advertise all kinds of products on TV.*

advice /ədˈvaɪs/ n. ★★★ conselho *My friend Callie always gives me good advice.*

afraid /əˈfreɪd/ adj. (never before noun) ★★★ medo *Carol is afraid of cockroaches.*

after /ˈæftər/ adv. conj. prep. ★★★ depois *I brush my teeth after eating.*

afternoon /ˌæftərˈnun/ n. ★★★ tarde *I have swimming classes in the afternoon.*

again /əˈgen/ adv. ★★★ novamente *I watched Twilight again yesterday.*

age /eɪdʒ/ n. ★★ idade; era *What's his age? He's eleven.*

air /er/ n. ★★★ ar **on the air** no ar *What's on the air on WXYZ? Sarah Jones's program.*

alive /əˈlaɪv/ adj. (never before noun) ★★★ vivo *Are your great-grandparents still alive?*

all /ɔl/ adv. deter. prep. pron. ★★★ tudo; todos *All my friends love sports.*

allow /əˈlaʊ/ v. ★★★ permitir *She allows her children to eat sweets on the weekend.*

alone /əˈloʊn/ adj. adv. ★★★ sozinho *Ady never stays alone at home.*

already /ɔlˈredi/ adv. ★★★ já *It's 7 p.m. and he is already sleeping.*

also /ˈɔlsoʊ/ adv. ★★★ também *Luisa is my sister, but she is also my friend.*

always /ˈɔlˌweɪz/ adv. ★★★ sempre *I always watch movies on the weekend.*

American /əˈmerɪkən/ adj. americano *Jess is an American teacher.*

amusing /əˈmjuzɪŋ/ adj. ★ divertido *This TV show is really amusing.*

ancient /ˈeɪnʃənt/ adj. antigo, muito velho *Rome is an ancient city.*

anonymously /əˈnɑnɪməsli/ adv. anonimamente *This letter was sent anonymously.*

another /əˈnʌðər/ det. pron. ★★★ outro *I need another pen; this one is not working.*

answer /ˈænsər/ n. v. ★★★ resposta; responder *The correct answer is B.*

antiperspirant /ˌæntiˈpɜrspərənt/ n. antitranspirante *I put on antiperspirant before exercising.*

any /ˈeni/ adv.det.pron. ★★★ algum, alguma *Do you have any money?*

anymore /ˌeniˈmɔr/ adv. ★★ não mais *I don't want to eat anymore.*

appear /əˈpɪr/ v. ★★★ parecer; aparecer *This exercise is not as difficult as it appears to be.*

appetizing /ˈæpəˌtaɪzɪŋ/ adj. apetitoso *These snacks are really appetizing.*

apple /ˈæp(ə)l/ n. ★★ maçã *Apples are my favorite fruit.*

appointment /əˈpɔɪntmənt/ n. ★★★ compromisso, horário, consulta *I have an appointment at the dentist tomorrow.*

appropriate /əˈproʊpriət/ adj. ★★★ apropriado *Fill in the blank with the appropriate word.*

arise /əˈraɪz/ v. ★★★ aparecer *This problem arises in a difficult time.*

around /əˈraʊnd/ adv.prep. ★★★ em volta de, em torno de *Let's walk around the park.*

arrive /əˈraɪv/ v. ★★★ chegar *The taxi will arrive at 8 o'clock.*

article /ˈɑrtɪk(ə)l/ n. ★★★ artigo *In English, a and an are articles.*

as /æz/ adv.prep.conj. ★★★ como *Ivan works as a designer.*

ask /æsk/ v. ★★★ perguntar *Can I ask you a question?*

at /æt/ prep. ★★★ em, às *We leave school at 1 o'clock.*

attend /əˈtend/ v. ★★★ frequentar, comparecer *We attend the same school and the same club.*

aunt /ænt/ n. ★★★ tia *My aunt's name is Jane.*

available /əˈveɪləb(ə)l/ adj. ★★★ disponível *This T-shirt is available in four colors.*

avoid /əˈvɔɪd/ v. ★★★ evitar *Vitor avoids eating meat.*

away /əˈweɪ/ adv. ★★★ para fora *Go away! I want to be alone.*

axe /æks/ n. ★ machado *They use the axe to cut the wood.*

axis /ˈæksɪs/ n. vetor *A graph is composed by a vertical and a horizontal axis.*

B

back /bæk/ n. ★★★ costas **be back** voltar *Said is back from Lebanon.*

background /ˈbækˌgraʊnd/ adj. ★★★ de fundo *The background image of this website is the company's logo.*

150   **Minidictionary**

backpack /ˈbækˌpæk/ n. mochila *I take this backpack everywhere I go.*

bad /bæd/ adj. ★★★ mau *The teacher is in a bad mood today.*

balloon /bəˈlun/ n. ★ balão *There are more than 50 balloons for the party decoration.*

band /bænd/ n. ★★★ banda *Roy plays in a jazz band.*

bank /bæŋk/ n. ★★★ banco *People working in a bank deal with money.*

bathroom /ˈbæθˌrum/ n. ★★ banheiro *Cristina's house has five bathrooms.*

bean /bin/ n. ★★ feijão, grãos *Rice and beans are a popular dish in Brazil.*

beautiful /ˈbjutɪf(ə)l/ adj. ★★★ bonita, bonito *This garden is really beautiful.*

because /bɪˈkɔz/ conj. ★★★ porque *The floor is wet because it rained.*

bed /bed/ n. ★★★ cama *Her bed is made of wood.*

bedtime /ˈbedˌtaɪm/ n. hora de dormir *It's bedtime. I'll read you a story.*

beef /bif/ n. ★★ bife *Vegetarians do not eat beef.*

before /bɪˈfɔr/ adv. ★★★ antes *Brush your teeth before going to bed.*

behind /bɪˈhaɪnd/ adv. prep. ★★★ atrás *The car is behind the tree.*

belief /bɪˈlif/ n. ★★★ crença *A gentleman does not disparage the beliefs of others.*

below /bɪˈləʊ/ adv. ★★★ abaixo, embaixo *The basement is below the house.*

benefit /ˈbenəfɪt/ n. ★★★ benefício *Reading brings you more benefits than you can imagine.*

best /best/ adj. ★★★ melhor *Rory and Jade are best friends.*

bet /bet/ n. v. ★★★ aposta, apostar *I bet you can't roll your tongue.*

better /ˈbetər/ adj. ★★★ melhor *Fernando is better in math than Cláudio.*

between /bɪˈtwin/ adv. ★★★ entre *The church is between the bank and the supermarket.*

big /bɪg/ adj. ★★★ grande *Russia is a very big country.*

bite /baɪt/ n. v. ★ mordida; morder *A puppy bite does not hurt.*

black /blæk/ n. ★★★ preto *Jim has back hair.*

blue /blu/ n. ★★★ azul *The sky is blue.*

board /bɔrd/ n. ★★★ quadro *Write your answer on the board.*

boarders internos **boarding school** colégio interno *These boarders live in the same school.*

body /ˈbɑdi/ n. ★★★ corpo *My body hurts because I exercised too much.*

boil /bɔɪl/ v. ★ ferver *Water boils at 100°C.*

book /bʊk/ n. ★★★ livro *This atlas is my least favorite book.*

booth /buð/ n. ★ cabine *Let's take a picture in this photo booth.*

born /bɔrn/ adj. ★★★ nascido *Lee was born in 1999.*

borrow /ˈbɔroʊ/ v. ★★★ tomar emprestado *Can I borrow your pen, please?*

both /boʊθ/ det. pron. ★★★ ambos *Elly and Ally are both my friends.*

bottle /ˈbɑt(ə)l/ n. ★★★ garrafa **bottle top** tampa de garrafa *The school recycles plastic bottles.*

bowl /boʊl/ n. ★★ tigela, pote *I have a bowl of cereal every morning.*

box /bɑks/ n. ★★★ caixa *Put the toys into the box.*

brand /brænd/ n. ★★ marca, logomarca *Lucas does not care about brands.*

bread /bred/ n. ★★★ pão *Ana loves bread with butter.*

breakfast /ˈbrekfəst/ n. ★★★ café da manhã *Breakfast is my favorite meal.*

bring /brɪŋ/ v. ★★★ trazer *You cannot bring pets to school.*

bristle /ˈbrɪs(ə)l/ n. cerda *These bristles are too old; I need a new toothbrush.*

brother /ˈbrʌðər/ n. ★★★ irmão *My brother is eight years old.*

brown /braʊn/ adj. ★★★ marrom *Lee's hair is brown.*

brunch /brʌntʃ/ n. refeição entre manhã e tarde, brunch *Our brunch generally starts at 11:00 on Sundays.*

brush /brʌʃ/ n. ★★★ escova **hair brush** escova de cabelo *Brush your hair and change your clothes.*

build /bɪld/ v. ★★★ construir *They are building a shopping mall near my house.*

bunk /bʌŋk/ n. beliche *My brother and I sleep in a bunk.*

bus /bʌs/ n. ★★★ ônibus *I take bus 58 to go to school.*

but /bʌt/ conj. ★★★ mas *It is hot, but windy.*

buy /baɪ/ v. ★★★ comprar *I buy food for the week on Thursdays.*

by /baɪ/ prep. ★★★ por **by the way** aliás *Helen and Hayley go to school by bus.*

bye /baɪ/ interj. ★★★ tchau *She said bye and left the room.*

C

cake /keɪk/ n. ★★★ bolo *Carrot cake is my favorite dessert.*

call /kɔːl/ v. ★★★ chamar; ligar *They call Rebecca Beckie.*

calm /kɑm/ adj. ★★ calmo *Monks are generally very calm.*

can /kæn/ v. n. ★★★ poder; lata *I have more than fifty cans of soda in my collection.*

capture /ˈkæptʃər/ v. ★★ capturar; tirar (foto) *The vets captured the tiger after his escape.*

car /kɑr/ n. ★★★ carro *My aunt's car is red.*

card /kɑː(r)d/ n. ★★★ cartão *I wrote a card for her birthday.*

care /ker/ n. ★★★ cuidado *You should handle your computer with care.*

carry /ˈkeri/ v. ★★★ carregar *Can you carry these bags?*

case /keɪs/ n. ★★★ caso *That's not the case.*

cat /kæt/ n. ★★★ gato *Felix is a black cat.*

cement /səˈment/ n. ★ cimento *This wall is made of bricks and cement.*

century /ˈsentʃəri/ n. ★★★ século *We are in the 21st century.*

certain /ˈsɜrt(ə)n/ adj. certo, seguro *I am certain he is in school today.*

Minidictionary

challenge /ˈtʃæləndʒ/ n. ★★★ desafio *Playing cards with my grandmother is a real challenge: she is so good!*

champion /ˈtʃæmpiən/ n. ★★★ campeão *Rodrigo is the champion of the school math competition.*

change /tʃeɪndʒ/ n. v. ★★★ trocar, troco *Change your clothes; it is cold!*

character /ˈkerəktər/ n. ★★★ personagem *Wonder Woman is a female character.* **characteristic** característica

charity /ˈtʃerəti/ n. ★★★ caridade *I donated the prize money to charity.*

chart /tʃɑrt/ n. ★★ gráfico, tabela *Complete the chart with information about you.*

check /tʃek/ v. ★★★ checar, marcar *Check the correct answers.*

cheese /tʃiz/ n. ★★ queijo *Mauricio loves ham and cheese sandwiches.*

chemical /ˈkemɪk(ə)l/ adj. ★★★ químico *Be careful! This chemical product is dangerous.*

chew /tʃu/ v. ★★ mascar *We can't chew gum in class.*

children /ˈtʃɪldrən/ plural of child crianças *Children must not work.*

Chinese /ˌtʃaɪˈniz/ n. adj. chinês *My parents love Chinese food.*

choose /tʃuz/ v. ★★★ escolher *I always choose pineapple ice cream.* **choice**

chuck /tʃʌk/ atirar, jogar *Chuck me the ball.*

cinnamon /ˈsɪnəmən/ n. canela *My mom decorates apple pies with cinnamon.*

circle /ˈsɜrk(ə)l/ v. ★ circular *Circle the correct answer.*

citizenship /ˈsɪtɪz(ə)nʃɪp/ n. ★ cidadania *Lilian has Italian citizenship.*

city /ˈsɪti/ n. ★★★ cidade *Rio de Janeiro is a beach city.*

class /klæs/ classe, turma escolar *Julio and Henrique are in the same class.*

clean /klin/ v. adj. ★★★ limpar, limpo *Clean your bedroom, please.*

clear /klɪr/ adj. claro *Are the instructions for the exercise clear?*

click /klɪk/ v. ★ clicar *Click here to go to the next page.*

close /kloʊz/ v. n. ★★★ fechar; próximo *It's windy; close the window, please.*

clothes /kloʊðz/ n. ★★★ roupas *Alice's clothes are new.*

clue /klu/ n. ★★ pista *The sentences have clues to discover the mystery.*

coffee /ˈkɑfi/ n. ★★★ café *Helen drinks coffee with milk every morning.*

coin /kɔɪn/ n. ★★ moeda *We have only three coins.*

cold /koʊld/ adj. ★★★ frio *Let's go inside; it's too cold here.*

collect /kəˈlekt/ v. ★★★ colecionar *Vinny collects stamps.* **collection** coleção **collector** colecionador

come /kʌm/ v. ★★★ vir *The stickers come with the album.*

complicated /ˈkɑmplɪˌkeɪtəd/ adj. ★★ complicado *This is a really complicated problem.*

compliment /ˈkɑmplɪmənt/ n. ★ cumprimento *He gave me a compliment for the composition.*

composition /ˌkɑmpəˈzɪʃ(ə)n/ n. ★★ redação, composição *We write compositions when we finish a unit of the book.*

computer lab laboratório de computação *Students have classes in the computer lab twice a week.*

concert /ˈkɑnsərt/ n. ★★ concerto, apresentação musical *Ricky sometimes goes to rock concerts.*

conclusion /kənˈkluʒ(ə)n/ n. ★★★ conclusão *Write a conclusion at the end of your composition.*

confusion /kənˈfjuʒ(ə)n/ n. ★★ confusão *The discussion ended in a lot of confusion.* **confused** confuso

consider /kənˈsɪdər/ v. ★★★ considerar *Deborah is considered to be the most intelligent student of our school.*

consist /kənˈsɪst/ v. ★★★ consistir *The activity consists of listening to the words and repeating them.*

consultant /kənˈsʌlt(ə)nt/ n. ★★ consultor *Sam's mother works as a financial consultant.*

consumer /kənˈsumər/ n. ★★★ consumidor *He is a great milk consumer; he drinks it everyday.* **consumerism** consumismo

contain /kənˈteɪn/ v. ★★★ conter *This bottle contains 500ml of water.*

contemporary /kənˈtempəˌreri/ adj. ★★★ contemporâneo *The two bands played in the 60s. They were contemporary.*

content /ˈkɑnˌtent/ n. ★★★ conteúdo *Go to the table of contents and check the number of the unit.*

contract /kənˈtrækt/ v. ★★ contratar *Our company contracts people from all over the world.*

convince /kənˈvɪns/ v. ★★★ convencer *They are trying to convince Sue to go to the movies with them.*

cook /kʊk/ v. ★★★ cozinhar *Marnie will cook something delicious tonight.*

cool /kul/ adj. ★★★ legal *The Oasis concert was really cool.*

copy /ˈkɑpi/ n. ★★★ copiar *Please, copy the answers in your notebooks.*

corporate /ˈkɔrp(ə)rət/ adj. ★★★ corporativo *My mother works in a corporate environment.*

corridor /ˈkɔrɪˌdɔr/ n. ★ corredor *There are posters and compositions on the walls of the corridor.*

cosmetics /kɑzˈmetɪks/ n. cosméticos *Barbra is crazy about cosmetics.*

cotton /ˈkɑt(ə)n/ n. ★★ algodão *All our clothes are made of cotton.*

could /kʊd/ modal ★★★ poderia *Could you give me the keys?*

course /kɔrs/ n. ★★★ curso *I attend English and Spanish courses at school.*

courtyard /ˈkɔrtˌjɑrd/ n. quintal, pátio *The kids go to the courtyard during the break.*

cousin /ˈkʌz(ə)n/ n. ★★★ primo, prima *There are in more than ten cousins in my family.*

cover /ˈkʌvər/ n. v. ★★★ capa; cobrir *The cover of this book is blue.*

cracker /ˈkrækər/ n. bolacha *They have tea and crackers as a snack.*

crazy /ˈkreɪzi/ adj. ★★ louco *Lucca is crazy about football.*

create /kriˈeɪt/ v. ★★★ criar They create many objects of art in this country. **creation** criação **creative** criativo

crowd /ˈkraʊd/ n. ★★★ multidão There is a crowd of fans outside the stadium. **crowded** lotado

curve /kɜrv/ n. ★★ curva Riding a bike in these curves is risky but nice.

cut /kʌt/ v. ★★★ cortar Cut this sheet of paper in three parts.

D

dance /dæns/ n. v. ★★★ dança; dançar Sheila and Sonja know how to dance really well. **dancer** dançarino

data /ˈdæt̬ə/ n. ★★★ dados I need to collect more data for my research.

date /deɪt/ n. ★★★ encontro, data Tomorrow is the final date for the contest applications.

day /deɪ/ n. ★★★ dia Bob loves sunny days.

dear /dɪr/ adj. ★★★ querido, querida Dear John, I miss you.

description /dɪˈskrɪpʃ(ə)n/ n. ★★★ descrição What's your job description?

detail /dɪˈteɪl/ n. ★ detalhe Pay attention to the details of the image.

dial /ˈdaɪəl/ v. ★ discar Dial 9 to call the reception.

diamond /ˈdaɪəmənd/ v. ★★ diamante Diamonds and grafitte come from carbon.

dictionary /ˈdɪkʃəˌneri/ n. ★★ dicionário Use this dictionary to check the meaning of the words.

dinner /ˈdɪnər/ n. ★★★ jantar We have dinner at 8:00 p.m.

direction /dɪˈrekʃ(ə)n/ n. ★★★ direção Can you give me the directions to school? **directly** diretamente

dirt /dɜrt/ n. ★ sujeira Clean that dirt from the table.

disabled /dɪˈseɪb(ə)ld/ adj. ★★ deficiente This parking space is for disabled drivers.

disadvantage /ˌdɪsədˈvæntɪdʒ/ n. ★★ desvantagem There are more advantages than disadvantages in doing exercise.

discard /dɪsˈkard/ v. descartar You should discard trash in the litter.

disorder /dɪsˈɔrdər/ n. ★★ distúrbio Insomnia is a sleeping disorder.

disparage /dɪˈsperɪdʒ/ v. ofender; falar mal They disparage anyone with ideas different from theirs.

dispose /dɪˈspoʊz/ v. ★★ descartar Dispose of your ice-cream wrapper in the trash can.

do /du/ v. ★★★ fazer Do your homework before watching TV.

doctor /ˈdaktər/ n. ★★★ doutor, médico Callie's brother is a children's doctor, he is a pediatrician.

dog /dɔg/ n. ★★★ cachorro Her dog's name is Rex.

doll /dal/ n. ★ boneca Susan is the name of my doll.

donate /ˈdoʊˌneɪt/ v. ★ doar I will donate the toys I do not like anymore. **donation** doação

door /dɔr/ n. ★★★ porta Come in and close the door.

dot /dat/ n. ★ ponto, pingo (do i) Cut along the dots.

doubt /daʊt/ n. ★★★ dúvida I have no doubts about his sports abilities.

draft /dræft/ n. ★★ rascunho This is just a draft; I'll give you the final composition tomorrow.

draw /drɔ/ v. ★★★ desenhar Draw your family tree in your notebook.

dried /draɪd/ adj. ★ seco Dried grapes are called raisins.

drink /drɪŋk/ v. n. ★★★ bebida, beber You should drink a lot of water every day.

drive /draɪv/ v. ★★★ dirigir Alice's father can drive cars and buses.

duration /dʊˈreɪʃ(ə)n/ n. duração The duration of a soccer game is about ninety minutes.

during /ˈdjʊərɪŋ/ prep. ★★★ durante The baby generally sleeps during the night.

E

each /itʃ/ det. pron. ★★★ cada Each apple costs 50 cents.

early /ˈɜrli/ adv. ★★★ cedo She wakes up early every day to go to school.

easy /ˈizi/ adj. ★★★ fácil, facilmente This exercise is not difficult; it is easy. **easily** facilmente

eat /it/ v. ★★★ comer Bruna eats salad every day.

effect /ɪˈfekt/ n. ★★★ efeito This movie is full of special effects.

egg /eg/ n. ★★★ ovo Pamela loves fried eggs.

elderly /ˈeldərli/ adj. idoso Elderly people have preference in public transportation.

empty /ˈempti/ adj. ★★★ vazio This bottle is empty. Can you fill it up with water?

energy /ˈenərdʒi/ n. ★★★ energia Turn off the lights to save energy.

engineering /ˌendʒɪˈnɪrɪŋ/ n. ★★★ engenharia Kara wants to work in the field of electronic engineering.

enjoy /ɪnˈdʒɔɪ/ v. ★★★ curtir, desfrutar Nina enjoys playing with dogs.

enough /ɪˈnʌf/ adv. ★★★ o suficiente Do not put sugar in the juice. It's sweet enough.

environment /ɪnˈvaɪrənmənt/ n. ★★★ meio ambiente Saving water is a way of protecting the environment.

especially /ɪˈspeʃ(ə)li/ adv. ★★★ especialmente I made a cake especially for my sister's birthday.

even /ˈiv(ə)n/ adv. ★★★ ímpar Three is an even number.

evening /ˈivnɪŋ/ n. ★★★ início da noite The movie starts at seven in the evening.

ever /ˈevər/ adv. ★★★ a qualquer momento For me, they are the best rock band ever.

every /ˈevri/ det. ★★★ todo Josh visits his grandparents every week.

exactly /ɪgˈzæk(t)li/ adv. ★★★ exatamente They are twins, but they are not exactly alike.

except /ɪkˈsept/ conj. prep. ★★★ exceto We all love coffee, except for Luiza.

excited /ɪkˈsaɪtəd/ adj. ★★ agitado, empolgado Flávio and Fred are really excited about the trip.

Minidictionary 153

Excuse me phrase com licença *Excuse me, where are the restrooms?*

exercise /ˈeksərˌsaɪz/ v. n. ★★★ exercitar-se; exercício *Louise exercises three times a week.*

expensive /ɪkˈspensɪv/ adj. ★★★ caro *This skirt is too expensive. I will buy the other one.*

extend /ɪkˈstend/ v. ★★★ extensão *Ask the teacher to extend the deadline.*

extract /ɪkˈstrækt/ v. ★★ excerto *Read the text extract and answer the questions.*

extreme /ɪkˈstrim/ adj. ★★ extremo *Any negative temperature is considered extreme in Brazil.*

eye /aɪ/ n. ★★★ olho *Mandy has blue eyes.*

eyebrow /ˈaɪˌbraʊ/ n. ★★ sobrancelha *She can move one eyebrow at a time.*

F

face /feɪs/ n. v. ★★★ face; encarar *Let's face the problem together.*

fact /fækt/ n. ★★★ fato *Read the story and summarize the facts.*

faith /feɪθ/ n. ★★★ fé *Some people have faith but are not religious.*

family /ˈfæm(ə)li/ n. ★★★ família *There are more than 60 members in my family.*

far /fɑr/ adj. ★★★ longe *Porto Velho is far from Curitiba.*

farm /fɑrm/ n. ★★★ fazenda *My grandparents live on a farm with lots of animals.*

fast /fæst/ adj. ★★★ rápido *Deer run really fast.*

feed /fid/ v. ★★★ alimentar *Cesar and Andre feed their cats twice a day.*

feel /fil/ v. ★★★ sentir *I feel sick. I want to stay home.* **feeling** sentimento

few /fju/ det. pron. ★★★ poucos *Students, you have just a few minutes to hand in your compositions.*

fiber /ˈfaɪbər/ n. ★★ fibra *These clothes are made of natural fiber.*

fight /faɪt/ v. n. ★★★ lutar, luta *Anderson Silva fights professionally.*

find /faɪnd/ v. ★★★ encontrar **find out** descobrir *I want to find out what time the film starts.*

fine /faɪn/ adj. ★★★ bem *I feel fine today.*

finger /ˈfɪŋɡər/ n. ★★★ dedo *We use the index finger to point to something we want to show.* **fingernail** dedo da mão

finish /ˈfɪnɪʃ/ v. ★★★ terminar *I finish my homework before watching TV.*

first /fɜrst/ numb. ★★★ primeiro *The first day of the week is Sunday.*

flat /flæt/ adj. ★★★ murcho *Your car's tire is flat. We must change it.*

flavor /ˈfleɪvər/ n. ★★ sabor *I want some ice cream. What flavor? Strawberry, please.*

flight /flaɪt/ n. ★★★ voo **flight attendant** comissário de bordo *Cecilia works a lot during the flights.*

flood /flʌd/ n. v. ★★ enchente; transbordar *In the summer, floods are common in Rio de Janeiro and São Paulo.*

dental floss expression fio dental *Use dental floss before or after brushing your teeth.*

flower /ˈflaʊr/ n. ★★★ flor *Roses, daisies, and poppies are beautiful flowers.*

fly /flaɪ/ v. ★★★ voar *Airplanes fly faster than birds.*

folk /foʊk/ n. adj. folclore; folclórico *Folk music is very traditional in this country.*

follow /ˈfɑloʊ/ v. ★★★ seguir *Follow good examples.*

food /fud/ n. ★★★ comida *Food is good for your body.*

foot /fʊt/ n. ★★★ pé *My foot hurts when I walk too much.* **feet** pés

for /fɔr/ prep. conj. ★★★ por; para *I want to order dinner for two, please.*

forget /fərˈɡet/ v. ★★★ esquecer *They never forget to call me on my birthday.*

form /fɔrm/ v. n. ★★★ formar; formulário *Fill in the form with information about you.*

free /friː/ adj. ★★ livre; grátis *In this restaurant, the dessert is free.*

fresh /freʃ/ adj. ★★★ fresco *I love eating fresh vegetables.*

Friday /ˈfraɪdeɪ/ n. ★★★ sexta-feira *Thank God it's Friday!*

friend /frend/ n. ★★★ amigo, amiga *Raquel is my best friend.*

from /frəm/ prep. ★★★ de *Hiro is from Japan.*

front /frʌnt/ n. adj. frente, da frente *Use the front door to enter the building.*

frustrated /ˈfrʌˌstreɪtəd/ adj. ★ frustrado *Will is frustrated because his team is out of the championship.*

fuel /ˈfjuəl/ n. ★★★ combustível *Our car needs some fuel.*

full /fʊl/ adj. ★★★ cheio *There is a box full of chocolates on the table.*

G

gang /ɡæŋ/ n. ★★ turma, grupo de amigos *There are more than five members in our gang.*

gate /ɡeɪt/ n. portão *Close the gate so the dog doesn't leave.*

gender /ˈdʒendər/ n. ★★ gênero (sexual) *What's the gender of your cat?*

genetics /dʒəˈnetɪks/ n. genética *If you have characteristics similar to your parents', it is due to genetics.*

genre /ˈʒɒnrə/ n. ★ gênero *Comedy is my favorite movie genre.*

geography /dʒiˈɑɡrəfi/ n. ★★ geografia *In geography classes we learn about places and peoples.*

German /ˈdʒɜrmən/ n. adj. alemão *Sausages and potatoes are a popular German dish.*

get /ɡet/ v. ★★★ obter *Buy a movie ticket and get another one for free.*

girl /ɡɜrl/ n. ★★★ menina *Lucy is a girl's name.*

girlfriend /ˈɡɜrlˌfrend/ n. ★★ namorada *She is not my girlfriend; she is just my friend.*

give /ɡɪv/ v. ★★★ dar *Give me the car keys.*

gland /ɡlænd/ n. glândula *Mariana has a problem with her thyroid gland.*

glass /ɡlɑːs/ n. ★★★ copo *Can I have a glass of water, please?*

154 **Minidictionary**

glossary /ˈglɒsəri/ n. glossário Check the glossary for the meaning of the words.

go back phrasal verb voltar I will go back to the house after the movie.

good /gʊd/ interj. ★★★ bom Ivan is a good friend.

grade /greɪd/ n. ★★ série I am in the 6th grade.

grain /greɪn/ n. ★★ grão At night, I prefer to eat grains and salad.

grandfather /ˈgræn(d)ˌfɑːðə(r)/ n. ★★ avô Our grandfather is 72 years old.

grandmother /ˈgræn(d)ˌmʌðər/ n. ★★ avó My grandmother lives with us.

grandparent /ˈgræn(d)ˌpeərənt/ n. ★ avó(s) Moe and Joe sometimes sleep at their grandparents' house.

grass /grɑːs/ n. ★★★ grama Do not step on the grass.

great /greɪt/ adj. ★★★ ótimo Lucca is a great student.

green /grin/ n. ★★★ verde Green is the color of the grass.

ground /graʊnd/ n. ★★★ chão Do not leave your bag on the ground.

guava /ˈgwɑːvə/ n. goiaba Guava is Adele's favorite tropical fruit.

guide /gaɪd/ n. ★★★ guia Eny is a tour guide in Argentina.

guitar /gɪˈtɑr/ n. ★★★ violão Alan plays the guitar very well.

gum /gʌm/ n. ★ gengiva Gingivitis is a gum disease.

H

habit /ˈhæbɪt/ n. ★★★ hábito, costume Drinking water is a healthy habit.

hair /her/ n. ★★★ cabelo His hair is red and short.

ham /hæm/ n. ★ presunto Ham and cheese sandwiches are common snack among children.

hand /hænd/ n. ★★★ mão I want to hold your hand.

handbook /ˈhæn(d)ˌbʊk/ n. caderno Copy the answers into your notebooks.

handkerchief /ˈhæŋkə(r)ˌtʃɪf/ n. ★ lenço If you sneeze, use a handkerchief.

handshake /ˈhæn(d)ˌʃeɪk/ n. aperto de mão A handshake is a polite compliment.

handwriting /ˈhændˌraɪtɪŋ/ n. letra cursiva Molly's handwriting is really beautiful; she studies caligraphy.

hang /hæŋ/ v. ★★★ pendurar Hang your coat on the hanger inside the wardrobe.

happen /ˈhæpən/ v. ★★★ acontecer Bienal do Livro happens every two years.

happy /ˈhæpi/ adj. ★★ feliz Happy is the opposite of sad.

happiness /ˈhæpinəs/ n. ★★ felicidade Happiness is the opposite of sadness.

hard /hɑrd/ adj. ★★★ duro This sofa is not comfortable; it is too hard.

head /hed/ n. cabeça **heads and tails** cara ou coroa This baby has such a small head!

health /helθ/ n. ★★★ saúde It is important to take care of your health.

hear /hɪə(r)/ v. ★★★ ouvir Can you hear that noise?

heart /hɑː(r)t/ n. ★★★ coração The heart is one of the most important organs in our bodies.

height /haɪt/ n. ★★★ altura What's your height?

hello /həˈləʊ/ interj. ★★★ olá Hello, my friend!

help /help/ v. ★★★ ajudar I need help with my homework.

hereditary /həˈredət(ə)ri/ adj. ★ hereditário My brother and my mother's eyes are green; it is hereditary.

hide-and-seek expression esconde-esconde Let's play hide-and-seek in the garden.

high /haɪ/ adj. ★★★ alto There are more than 50 floors in this building; it is very high.

highlight /ˈhaɪˌlaɪt/ v. n. ★★ destacar; destaque Highlight the words you do not understand from the text.

history /ˈhɪst(ə)ri/ n. ★★★ história Alix is my history teacher.

hobby /ˈhɑbi/ n. ★ atividade de lazer Reading is my favorite hobby.

hold /hoʊld/ v. ★★★ segurar Hold your breath and jump into the water.

hole /hoʊl/ n. ★★★ buraco Be careful with the hole in the ground.

home /hoʊm/ n. ★★★ lar, casa What time are you coming home? **homeless** sem teto

honey /ˈhʌni/ n. ★ mel Yogurt with honey is a traditional Greek dessert.

horse /hɔː(r)s/ n. ★★★ cavalo Riding horses is one of Paula's pastimes.

hot /hɑt/ adj. ★★★ quente **hot dog** cachorro-quente This tea is really hot.

hour /aʊr/ n. ★★★ hora I will meet you at the movie in an hour.

house /haʊs/ n. ★★★ casa My house is the green one.

how /haʊ/ adv. conj. ★★★ como How are you?

human /ˈhjuːmən/ adj. ★★★ humano Dogs generally like human beings.

hungry /ˈhʌŋgri/ adj. ★★ faminto I'm so hungry; I need to eat.

hygiene /ˈhaɪdʒiːn/ n. ★ higiene Brushing your teeth is part of your hygiene.

I

idea /aɪˈdiə/ n. ★★★ ideia Your idea for the project is great!

if /ɪf/ conj. ★★★ se Call me if you need anything.

impressive /ɪmˈpresɪv/ adj. ★★ impressionante He did an impressive job with those kids.

inappropriate /ˌɪnəˈprəʊpriət/ adj. ★★ inapropriado Your clothes are inappropriate to enter school.

included /ɪnˈkluːdəd/ adj. incluído The CD is included in the book.

index /ˈɪndeks/ n. ★★★ índice Check the index to see the correct pages of the book.

infer /ɪnˈfɜː(r)/ v. ★ inferir Look at the pictures and infer what they are talking about.

inform /ɪnˈfɔː(r)m/ v. ★★★ informar Inform your parents about the meeting next week. **information** informação

Minidictionary 155

inside /ˈɪnˌsaɪd/ adj. adv. pron. ★★★ dentro *There are eight fish inside this aquarium.*

interaction /ˌɪntərˈækʃ(ə)n/ n. ★★ interação *I enjoy the interaction with my friends and cousins.*

interesting /ˈɪntrəstɪŋ/ adj. ★★★ interessante *This new movie is very interesting.* **interest** interesse

interview /ˈɪntərˌvju/ n. ★★★ entrevista *Justin Bieber's interview is at 4 o'clock.*

into /ˈɪntu/ prep. ★★★ em, no, na *He jumped into the river.*

investigate /ɪnˈvestɪgeɪt/ v. ★★★ investigar *The police will investigate this case.*

invitation /ˌɪnvɪˈteɪʃ(ə)n/ n. ★★ convite *I have an invitation for Bel's birthday.* **invite** convidar

iron /ˈaɪə(r)n/ n. ★★ ferro *The school gate is made of iron.*

island /ˈaɪlənd/ n. ★★★ ilha *Fernando de Noronha is an island in Brazil.*

J

jacket /ˈdʒækɪt/ n. ★★★ jaqueta *I want a jean jacket as a birthday present.*

jam /dʒæm/ n. ★ geleia *My grandmother makes delicious strawberry jam.*

job /dʒɒb/ n. ★★★ trabalho *Heloisa leaves her job at 6 o'clock.*

joke /dʒəʊk/ n. ★★ piada *Comedians invent jokes very easily.*

journey /ˈdʒɜː(r)ni/ n. ★★★ viagem, trajetória, jornada *Life is a journey: enjoy it.*

judge /dʒʌdʒ/ n. ★★★ juiz *The judge has the final word.*

juice /dʒuːs/ n. ★★ suco *Sometimes we drink orange juice for breakfast.*

just /dʒʌst/ adv. ★★★ só *He is not my brother, he is just a friend.*

K

keep /kip/ v. ★★★ manter *Keep calm and carry on.*

kid /kɪd/ n. ★★★ criança *The kids are in the garden.*

kidnap /ˈkɪdnæp/ v. ★ sequestrar *In that movie, they kidnap the president's family.*

kind /kaɪnd/ adj. ★★★ gentil; tipo **kind of** tipo de *The waiter was very kind to us.*

knife /naɪf/ n. ★★★ faca *Use a knife to cut the bread.*

know /nəʊ/ v. ★★★ saber *I know how to draw a castle.*

L

lady /ˈleɪdi/ n. ★★★ senhora *That lady is Carrie's grandmother.*

large /lɑː(r)dʒ/ adj. ★★★ grande *I want a large cup of coffee.*

last /læst/ v. adj. adv. ★★★ durar, último *My sister is on the last train to Brighton.*

laugh /lɑːf/ v. n. ★★ rir; riso; risada *When I tell a joke, my brother laughs.*

lead /liːd/ v. ★★★ liderar *The captain leads the team.*

learn /lɜː(r)n/ v. ★★★ aprender *We learn English at school.*

leave /liːv/ v. ★★★ deixar, partir *The bus will leave the station at 4 o'clock.*

left /left/ adj. ★★★ esquerda *Paul writes with his left hand.*

lend /lend/ v. ★★ emprestar *Can you lend me your pen?*

lentil /ˈlentɪl/ n. lentilha *It is a tradition to eat lentils on New Year's Eve.*

less /les/ adv. prep. pron. ★★★ menos *There is less sugar in juice than in soft drinks.*

let /let/ v. ★★★ deixar *Open the window and let the sun in.*

letter /ˈletər/ n. ★★★ carta **letter paper** papel de carta *Laurie sometimes receives letters.*

library /ˈlaɪbrəri/ n. ★★★ biblioteca *This library has thousands of books.* **librarian** bibliotecário

life /laɪf/ n. ★★★ vida *Your life starts when you are born and finishes when you die.*

light /laɪt/ n. adj. ★★★ luz, claridade; leve, claro *Turn on the lights; it is really dark in here.*

like /laɪk/ v. ★★★ gostar *Mirian really likes cats.*

line /laɪn/ n. ★★★ linha *Write your name in the last line.*

link /lɪŋk/ n. v. link *Click on the link to see the video.*

listen /ˈlɪs(ə)n/ v. ★★★ ouvir *Listen to your teacher.*

litter /ˈlɪtə(r)/ n. ★ lixo *The rivers of São Paulo are full of litter.*

little /ˈlɪt(ə)l/ adj. ★★★ pequeno *There is little room for people in the kitchen.*

live /lɪv/ v. ★★★ viver *Our neighbors live next door.*

liver /ˈlɪvə(r)/ n. ★ fígado *Hepatitis is a disease of the liver.*

living /ˈlɪvɪŋ/ adj. ★★★ de viver; vivo *Living conditions are terrible when you do not have potable water.*

lizard /ˈlɪzə(r)d/ n. ★ lagarto *Lizards are a kind of reptile.*

look /lʊk/ v. n. ★★★ olhar *Look at the sentence and find the mistake.*

lose /luːz/ v. ★★★ perder *They practice so hard because they cannot lose this game.*

lost /lɒst/ adj. ★★ perdido *I am lost. Can you help me find my house?*

(a) lot (of) phrase muito (de) *We need a lot of sugar to make this cake.*

loud /laʊd/ adj. ★★ alto (som) *This radio is too loud; turn it down.*

love /lʌv/ n. v. ★★★ amor; amar *Dogs love playing.*

low /ləʊ/ adj. ★★★ baixo *The prices are really low in this store.*

luck /lʌk/ n. ★★ sorte *Good luck on your exams!*

lunch /lʌntʃ/ n. ★★★ almoço **lunch worker, -lady, -man** cantineira, cantineiro *The lunch worker prepares our snacks at school.*

M

made /meɪd/ adj. feito *This box is made of wood.*

magazine /ˈmægəˌzin/ n. ★★★ revista *Seventeen is a magazine for teenagers.*

main /meɪn/ adj. ★★★ principal *The teacher's room is in the main building.*

make /meɪk/ v. ★★★ fazer *Let's make a carrot cake for dessert.*

male /meɪl/ adj. ★★★ masculino *If you are a boy, go to the male restroom.*

mall /mɔl/ n. ★★ centro de compras *We can ride a bike or go to the shopping mall.*

management /ˈmænɪdʒmənt/ n. ★★★ gerenciamento *Time management helps you with your studies.*

manner /ˈmænə(r)/ n. ★★★ maneira, jeito *Show me the correct manner to play the flute.*

many /ˈmeni/ adv. ★★★ muitos *There are many kinds of fish in the city aquarium.*

mark /mɑː(r)k/ v. n. ★★★ marcar; marca, nota *Mark the correct answers.*

married /ˈmærid/ adj. ★★★ casado *Our geography teacher is married to our PE instructor.*

martial arts expression artes marciais *Kelly practices martial arts twice a week.*

mass /mæs/ n. ★★★ missa *They go to mass on Sundays.*

match /mætʃ/ v. n. ★★★ ligar, conectar; partida, palito de fósforo *Match the words to the pictures they represent.*

math /mæθ/ n. ★ matemática *Harry doesn't think math is difficult.*

matter /ˈmætər/ n. ★★★ situação, problema *What's the matter? Are you OK?*

may /meɪ/ modal ★★★ poder *May I go to the restroom?*

maybe /ˈmeɪbi/ adv. ★★★ talvez *Maybe I am getting the flu. I feel hot.*

meal /mil/ n. ★★★ refeição *Breakfast is the first meal we have in a day.*

mean /min/ v. ★★★ significar *What does "book" mean?*

microorganism /ˌmaɪkroʊˈɔrɡəˌnɪzəm/ n. micro-organismo *You can only see a microorganism through a microscope.*

middle /ˈmɪd(ə)l/ n. ★★★ meio *His middle name is Silva; his full name is Joe da Silva Jones.*

midnight /ˈmɪdˌnaɪt/ n. ★★ meia--noite *You should go to bed before midnight.*

milk /mɪlk/ n. ★★★ leite *I hate drinking milk without chocolate.*

mint /mɪnt/ n. menta *This chocolate with mint is delicious.*

mixture /ˈmɪkstʃər/ n. ★★★ mistura *Her face showed a mixture of fear and excitement.*

monastery /ˈmɑnəˌsteri/ n. monastério *Monks live in monasteries.*

Monday /ˈmʌnˌdeɪ/ n. ★★★ segunda-feira *Our classes start on Monday.*

money /ˈmʌni/ n. ★★★ dinheiro *I need money to buy popcorn.*

monk /mʌŋk/ n. ★ monge *Is your uncle a monk or a priest?*

month /mʌnθ/ n. ★★★ mês *January is the first month of the year.*

more /mɔr/ adv. pron. ★★★ mais *I want more rice, please.*

morning /ˈmɔrnɪŋ/ n. ★★★ manhã *I wake up at 6 in the morning.*

most /moʊst/ adv. ★★★ superlativo de much e many *Bruno is the most intelligent of my friends.*

mother /ˈmʌðər/ n. ★★★ mãe *My aunt is my cousin's mother.*

motivated /ˈmoʊtɪˌveɪtəd/ adj. motivado *Harry is really motivated for his guitar classes.* **motivation** motivação

mouse /maʊs/ n. ★★ rato *A cat generally runs after a mouse.* **pl. mice**

mouth /maʊθ/ n. ★★★ boca *You should cover your mouth when you sneeze.* **mouthwash** enxágue bucal

move /muv/ v. ★★★ mover; mudar-se *Our neighbors will move to another city.*

movie theaters expression sala de cinema *The film is in more than 20 movie theaters.*

multiply /ˈmʌltɪˌplaɪ/ v. ★ multiplicar *Multiply these two numbers to get the result.*

must /mʌst/ modal ★★★ dever *You must do your homework.*

my /maɪ/ deter. ★★★ meu *My name is Sue.*

N

nail /neɪl/ n. ★★ unha *You should not bite your nails.*

name /neɪm/ n. ★★★ nome **last name** sobrenome *Sarandon is her last name.*

near /nɪr/ adj. adv. prep. perto, próximo *Niterói is near Rio de Janeiro.*

necessary /ˈnesəs(ə)ri/ adj. ★★★ necessário *It is necessary to close your eyes to sleep.*

need /nid/ v. ★★★ precisar *We need milk to make this cake.*

never /ˈnevər/ adv. ★★★ nunca *You should never cross the street when the light is red.*

new /njuː/ adj. ★★★ novo *I've just bought a new pair of sneakers.*

news /njuːz/ n. ★★★ notícias *I have good news for you.*

newspaper /ˈnuzˌpeɪpər/ n. ★★★ jornal, periódico *Celia reads the newspaper every morning.*

next /nekst/ adj. adv. det. pron. ★★★ próximo, próxima *I sit next to him.*

nice /naɪs/ adj. ★★★ legal *He is a nice teacher.*

night /naɪt/ n. ★★★ noite *Good night, see you tomorrow.*

nobody /ˈnoʊˌbɑdi/ pron. ★★★ ninguém *Nobody knows where Carly is.*

noise /nɔɪz/ n. ★★★ barulho *Stop that noise; I want to sleep.*

none /nʌn/ adv. ★★★ nenhum *None of the contestants is a singer, they are all composers.*

noodle /ˈnud(ə)l/ n. macarrão instantâneo *Noodles are a fast meal.*

nose /noʊz/ n. ★★★ nariz *When Sarah takes an airplane, her nose bleeds.*

note /noʊt/ n. ★★★ anotação *Pay attention and take notes.*

notice /ˈnoʊtɪs/ v. ★★★ perceber, reparar *Notice the stress of the words.*

noun /naʊn/ n. ★ substantivo *An adjective qualifies a noun.*

now /naʊ/ adv. ★★★ agora *Now you can go home.*

number /ˈnʌmbər/ n. ★★★ número *Seven is my lucky number.*

nut /nʌt/ n. ★★ noz *Chocolate with nuts is excellent.*

Minidictionary 157

O

of /əv/ prep. ★★★ de *Blue is the color of the sky.*

offer /ˈɔfər/ v. n. ★★★ oferecer, oferta *Today, the snack bar has a special offer.*

often /ˈɔf(ə)n/ adv. ★★★ frequente, frequentemente *Leonard often goes to the cinema.*

old /oʊld/ adj. ★★★ velho *My teacher is not very old.*

olive oil n. azeite de oliva *Ivan likes olive oil in his green salad.*

on /ɔn/ adv. prep. ★★★ em, no, na *The book is on the table.*

once /wʌns/ adv. ★★★ uma vez *Once I watched a soccer game in a stadium.*

one /wʌn/ numb. ★★★ um *One is the name of a Beatles album.*

only /ˈəʊnli/ adv. ★★★ só, somente *This restroom is only for women.*

open /ˈəʊpən/ v. n. ★★★ abrir; aberto *Open your mouth and show me your tongue.*

opportunity /ˌɑpərˈtunəti/ n. ★★★ oportunidade *There are great opportunities for artists in that area.*

optical /ˈɒptɪk(ə)l/ adj. ★ ótico *He has a problem in his optical nerve.*

or /ɔr/ conj. ★★ ou *Do you want an orange or an apple?*

orange /ˈɔrəndʒ/ n. ★★ laranja *Orange is the name of a color and a fruit.*

order /ˈɔː(r)də(r)/ v. n. ★★★ pedir; pedido, ordem *Let's order some pizza for dinner.*

our /aʊr/ poss. det. ★★★ nosso, nossa *Our house is the one on the corner.*

out /aʊt/ adv. prep. ★★★ fora *Fernando is out of town today.*

outside /ˌaʊtˈsaɪd/ adj. adv. prep. ★★★ externo; do lado de fora; fora *They will build a factory outside town.*

over /ˈəʊvə(r)/ adv. prep. ★★★ sobre, por cima *There is a bridge over the river.*

overcome /ˌəʊvə(r)ˈkʌm/ v. ★★ superar *What can I do to overcome my fear of heights?*

overweight /ˌoʊvərˈweɪt/ adj. acima do peso *You are overweight; you should go on a diet.*

own /əʊn/ adj. pron. ★★★ próprio *Dan has his own bedroom.*

P

paint /peɪnt/ v. n. ★★★ pintar; tinta *Let's paint the fence.*

pair /peə(r)/ n. ★★★ par *Do the activity in pairs.*

panic /ˈpænɪk/ n. ★★ pânico *In case of fire, follow the rules and do not panic.*

paper /ˈpeɪpər/ n. ★★★ papel *Write your name on a piece of paper.*

paragraph /ˈperəˌgræf/ n. ★★★ parágrafo *A text is generally divided into paragraphs.*

parent /ˈperənt/ n. ★★★ pais *My parents are divorced.*

park /pɑrk/ n. ★★★ parque *This park closes at 8 o'clock.*

partner /ˈpɑrtnər/ n. ★★★ parceiro, colega, dupla *Ned and Alice are partners; they always work together.*

party /ˈpɑrti/ n. ★★★ festa **house party** festa em casa *My friend is throwing a house party tonight.*

pass /pɑːs/ v. ★★★ passar *Aryane studies a lot because she wants to pass the exam.*

passage /ˈpæsɪdʒ/ n. ★★★ excerto de texto *Read the passage and discuss the ideas with a classmate.*

passenger /ˈpæsɪndʒə(r)/ ★★★ n. passageiro *All passengers must pay for the ticket.*

paste /peɪst/ v. colar *Paste the pictures onto the albun.*

pay /peɪ/ v. ★★★ pagar **pay attention** prestar atenção *Pay attention to the teacher's instructions.*

peck /pek/ v. bicar; bicada *The woodpecker pecks holes in trees.*

peelings /ˈpiːlɪŋz/ n. cascas (de frutas ou vegetais) *This dessert is made of orange peelings.*

pepper /ˈpepər/ n. ★ pimenta *Renata is allergic to pepper; she can't eat it.*

perform /pə(r)ˈfɔː(r)m/ v. ★★★ performar, apresentar *The band will perform five shows next month.*

period /ˈpɪriəd/ n. ★★★ ponto final, período *Use a period at the end of the sentence.*

person /ˈpɜː(r)s(ə)n/ n. ★★★ pessoa (pessoas) *Barack Obama is a famous person all over the world.* **people** pessoas

pet /pet/ n. ★★ animal de estimação *He has a fish for a pet.*

physical /ˈfɪzɪk(ə)l/ adj. ★★★ físico *Physical exercise is good for your body and mind.*

pick /pɪk/ v. ★★★ pegar, escolher *Pick the T-shirt you prefer and I will pick the other one.*

picture /ˈpɪktʃər/ n. ★★★ ilustração, foto *Look at the pictures on page 56.*

piece /pis/ n. ★★★ pedaço *Write your name on a piece of paper.*

pig /pɪg/ n. ★★ porco *There are more than 20 pigs on that farm.*

piper /ˈpaɪpə(r)/ n. músico que toca flauta *That piper plays in three bands.*

place /pleɪs/ n. ★★★ lugar, local *I know where this place is; it's near my house.*

play /pleɪ/ v. ★★★ jogar, tocar *Let's play volleyball at the beach.* **player** jogador

please /pliz/ interj. ★★★ por favor *Please, come here.*

plus /plʌs/ adj. conj. prep. ★★★ mais *Five plus two is equal to seven.*

polite /pəˈlaɪt/ adj. ★ educado *You must be more polite to your customers.*

pollute /pəˈluːt/ v. ★ poluir *We should not pollute the rivers.*

pomegranate /ˈpɒmɪˌgrænət/ n. romã *Pomegranate is how we say romã in English.*

powder /ˈpaʊdə(r)/ n. ★★ pó, talco, pó de arroz *This detergent is available in both liquid and powder forms.*

practice /ˈpræktɪs/ v. n. ★★ praticar; prática *Let's practice this conversation in pairs.*

prefer /prɪˈfɜː(r)/ v. ★★★ preferir *Ivan prefers vegetables to chicken.*

pregnant /ˈpregnənt/ adj. ★★ grávida *My sister is four months pregnant.*

Minidictionary

presentation /ˌprez(ə)nˈteɪʃ(ə)n/ n. ★★★ apresentação *The teacher liked our presentation a lot.*

principal /ˈprɪnsəp(ə)l/ n. ★★ diretor *Our tests are in the principal's room.*

print /prɪnt/ v. n. ★★★ imprimir; impressão *Print six copies of this document.*

priority /praɪˈɒrəti/ n. ★★★ prioridade *Erradicating poverty must be a top priority in developing countries.*

private /ˈpraɪvət/ adj. ★★★ privado *This is a private call; please do not listen.*

professor /prəˈfesə(r)/ n. ★★ professor universitário *Robert is a professor at the university.*

proof /pruːf/ n. adj. ★★ prova; à prova de *Do you have any proof that this is true?*

properly /ˈprɒpə(r)li/ adv. ★★ apropriadamente, corretamente *You are not properly dressed for this weather.*

provide /prəˈvaɪd/ v. ★★★ prover *This meal provides all the energy you need for the exercise.*

protect /prəˈtekt/ v. ★★★ proteger *Wear a helmet to protect your head.* **protection** proteção

psychology /saɪˈkɒlədʒi/ n. ★★ psicologia *My aunt studied psychology.*

pure /pjʊr/ adj. ★★★ puro *This mousse is made of pure chocolate.*

purple /ˈpɜrp(ə)l/ adj. ★ roxo *Amethyst is a purple gem.*

put /pʊt/ v. ★★★ pôr, colocar *Put your notebook on the table.*

R

race /reɪs/ n. ★★★ raça *We do not discriminate on the basis of race or gender.*

raise /reɪz/ v. ★★★ levantar *Raise your hand to ask a question.*

rarely /ˈrerli/ adv. ★★★ raramente *I rarely drink soda during the week.*

reading /ˈridɪŋ/ n. ★★★ leitura *Reading is a great pastime.*

receiver /rɪˈsivər/ n. ★★ fone *We use receivers to make phone calls.*

recipe /ˈresəpi/ n. ★★ receita (culinária) *I know an easy apple pie recipe.*

recommendation /ˌrekəmenˈdeɪʃ(ə)n/ n. ★★ recomendação *Do you have any special recommendation?*

record /rɪˈkɔrd/ v. ★★★ gravar *This is the studio they use to record the songs.*

recycled /riˈsaɪk(ə)ld/ adj. ★ reciclado *This notebook is made of recycled paper.*

red /red/ adj. ★★★ vermelho *You must stop when the light is red.*

reduce /rɪˈdus/ v. ★★★ reduzir *This store reduces all the prices in January.*

refresh /rɪˈfreʃ/ v. refrescar *Drink some water to refresh.*

rehearsal /rɪˈhɜrs(ə)l/ n. ★ ensaio *We have several rehearsals before the presentation.*

remember /rɪˈmembər/ v. ★★★ lembrar *Remember to call me when you get there.*

reproducible /ˌriprəˈdusəb(ə)l/ adj. reproduzível *These grammar exercises are reproducible.*

request /rɪˈkwest/ n. ★★★ pedido *It is important to make requests in a polite way.*

research /rɪˈsɜrtʃ/ n. ★★★ pesquisa *We have to do a research about tropical fruits.*

responsibility /rɪˌspɒnsəˈbɪləti/ n. ★★★ responsabilidade *Doing the homework is the responsibility of the student.* **responsible** responsável

rice /raɪs/ n. ★★ arroz *Harry eats rice and beans every day.*

ride /raɪd/ v. n. ★★★ dirigir, conduzir; corrida *Ana and Harry ride their bikes in the park every day.*

right /raɪt/ adv. ★★★ certo, direito *Our teacher is the one on the right in the photo.*

rim /rɪm/ n. ★ borda *This glass is broken on the rim.*

ring /rɪŋ/ n. ★★★ anel *Candy has a collection of rings.*

road /roʊd/ n. ★★★ rua *They live on Abbey Road.*

robot /ˈroʊˌbɒt/ n. ★ robô *In the future, robots will be able to interact with us.*

rock /rɑk/ n. ★★★ pedra *This beach is full of rocks.*

roll /roʊl/ v. n. ★★★ enroladinho; enrolar *I love ham and cheese rolls.*

room /rum/ n. ★★★ quarto, sala, espaço *There is plenty of room in this garden.*

routine /ˌruˈtin/ n. ★★ rotina *We have a strict routine at school.*

row /roʊ/ n. ★★★ fileira *This class has five rows.*

rule /rul/ n. ★★★ regra *Pay attention to the rules of the game.*

run /rʌn/ v. ★★★ correr *Our friends run 10 kilometers a day.*

S

safe /seɪf/ adj. ★★★ seguro *It is safe to use banks through the Internet.* **safety** segurança

(for the) sake (of) phrase pelo bem de *He should be careful for his own sake.*

salt /sɔlt/ n. ★★ sal *You do not have to add salt to food.*

same /seɪm/ adj. adv. pron. ★★★ mesmo *We have the same name: we are both called Raj.*

sample /ˈsæmp(ə)l/ n. ★★★ amostra *We conducted a survey with a sample of 100 students.*

Saturday /ˈsætərˌdeɪ/ n. ★★★ sábado *We do not go to school on Saturdays.*

say /seɪ/ v. ★★★ dizer *Say a number between one and ten.*

scent /sent/ n. ★ cheiro *The scent of this parfume is really sweet.*

schedule /ˈskedʒul/ n. ★★ horário, cronograma *Check this schedule for your next class.*

school /skul/ n. ★★★ escola **school grade** ano escolar **school office** secretaria da escola *Where is your school?*

science /ˈsaɪəns/ n. ★★★ ciência *We go to the lab in our science class.*

sea /si/ n. ★★★ mar *Ruy loves swimming in the sea.*

seat /sit/ n. v. ★★ assento; sentar *Go back to your seats and do the activity.*

second /ˈsekənd/ numb. ★★★ segundo *Second prize is a bicycle.*

Minidictionary 159

security /sɪˈkjʊrəti/ n. ★★★ segurança *If you hear something strange, call security.*

see /si/ v. ★★★ ver *I love to see the sun rising.*

selfish /ˈsɛlfɪʃ/ adj. ★ egoísta *Selfish people generally do not have many friends.*

sell /sɛl/ v. ★★★ vender *They sell movie tickets at this store.*

seriously /ˈsɪriəsli/ adv. ★★★ seriamente *They were discussing the matter seriously.*

serve /sɜrv/ v. ★★★ servir *Paul will serve in the Army.*

service /ˈsɜrvɪs/ n. ★★★ serviço *This is a self-service laundromat.*

set /sɛt/ v. ★★★ ajustar *Set the alarm to 9 o'clock.*

share /ʃɛr/ v. ★★★ dividir *Let's share this piece of cake.*

shine /ʃaɪn/ v. ★★ brilhar *The sun shines all through the summer.* **shining** brilhante

shoe /ʃu/ n. ★★★ sapato *Lucy loves her red shoes.*

shop /ʃɑp/ v. ★★★ comprar *We ate lunch at a little coffee shop.* **shopping** compras

short /ʃɔrt/ adj. ★★★ curto *Henry's hair is short.*

should /ʃʊd/ modal ★★★ deveria *We all should study before the exam.*

shout /ʃaʊt/ v. ★★★ gritar *Shout "bingo" when you finish the game.*

show /ʃoʊ/ v. ★★★ mostrar, apresentar *Show me your cards.*

shower /ˈʃaʊər/ n. ★★ chuveiro *The shower is located in the bathroom.*

sign /saɪn/ v. n. ★★★ assinar; sinal *Sign your name at the bottom of the page.*

since /sɪns/ adv. conj. prep. ★★★ desde *Ally has played tennis since 2009.*

sing /sɪŋ/ v. ★★★ cantar *Aretha sings in a jazz band.* **singer** cantor, cantora

sister /ˈsɪstər/ n. ★★★ irmã *Belle is Becky's sister.*

skip /skɪp/ v. ★ pular *Skip this track and listen to the next song.*

slam /slæm/ v. ★★ bater (a porta) *Don't slam the door.*

sleep /slip/ v. ★★★ dormir *Children sleep more hours than adults.*

slice /slaɪs/ n. ★★ fatia *I want to eat a slice of cake.*

small /smɔl/ adj. ★★★ pequeno *I have a small doll called Poppy.*

smell /smɛl/ v. n. ★★ cheirar; cheiro *I love the smell of apple pies.* **smelly** fedido

smoke /smoʊk/ v. n. ★★ fumar; fumaça *Where there is smoke, there is fire.*

sneaker /ˈsnikər/ n. tênis *Mirna needs a new pair of sneakers to train.*

sneeze /sniz/ v. espirrar *Cover your mouth when you sneeze.*

so /soʊ/ adv. conj. ★★★ tão *He is so smart! I'm impressed.*

soap /soʊp/ n. ★★ sabão **soap opera** novela *Use this soap to wash your face.*

soccer /ˈsɑkər/ n. ★ futebol *Soccer is a popular sport in Brazil.*

society /səˈsaɪəti/ n. ★★★ sociedade *We live in a complex society.*

sock /sɑk/ n. ★ meia *There is a hole in your sock.*

soil /sɔɪl/ n. ★★★ solo *Plant the seeds in the soil.*

soldier /ˈsoʊldʒər/ n. ★★★ soldado *Soldiers have to do a lot of exercise.*

solution /səˈluʃ(ə)n/ n. ★★★ solução *Finding a solution is never easy.*

solve /sɑlv/ v. ★★★ solucionar *Let's solve this problem together.*

some /sʌm/ adv. det. pron. ★★★ algum *We need some sugar for the cake.*

someone /ˈsʌmwʌn/ pron. ★★★ alguém *Someone is knocking on the door.*

sometimes /ˈsʌmtaɪmz/ adv. ★★★ às vezes *Sometimes I study, sometimes I play sports.*

son /sʌn/ n. ★★★ filho *Joseph is Hay's son.*

song /sɔŋ/ n. ★★★ canção *We writes songs and poems.*

sorry /ˈsɔri/ adj. ★★★ (sentir muito) *I'm sorry you have the flu.*

sound /saʊnd/ n. ★★★ som **sound effect** efeito sonoro *The sound of rain calms her down.*

space /speɪs/ n. ★★★ espaço *There is no space on this flash drive.*

speak /spik/ v. ★★★ falar *Vicky speaks Portuguese and Italian.*

speaker /ˈspikər/ n. ★★★ auto-falante *This computer has two speakers.*

special /ˈspɛʃ(ə)l/ adj. ★★★ especial *They have special desserts in this restaurant.*

specific /spəˈsɪfɪk/ adj. ★★★ específico *This restroom is specific for people with special needs.*

spelling /ˈspɛlɪŋ/ n. ★ grafia *What's the correct spelling of this word?*

spend /spɛnd/ v. ★★★ gastar *He spends a lot on food.*

stand /stænd/ v. n. ★★★ ficar, permanecer; estande *Stand here by my side.*

star /stɑr/ n. ★★★ estrela *In the countryside, we can see lots of stars at night.*

start /stɑrt/ v. ★★★ começar *The game starts at 5 o'clock.*

state /steɪt/ n. ★★★ estado *Brazil is divided into 26 states.*

station /ˈsteɪʃ(ə)n/ n. ★★★ estação *The bus station is in the city center.*

stay /steɪ/ v. ★★★ ficar *I stay in school until 1 o'clock.*

stencil /ˈstɛns(ə)l/ n. estêncil *We always decorate the walls with stencil.*

step /stɛp/ n. ★★★ passo; degrau *There are 200 steps in this staircase.*

stick /stɪk/ v. ★★★ grudar *Stick the posters on the wall.*

still /stɪl/ adv. adj. ★★★ ainda; parado *They still live in the same house.*

stinky /ˈstɪŋki/ adj. fedido *This cheese is stinky.*

stomach /ˈstʌmək/ n. ★★ estômago *My stomach hurts so much!*

stop /stɑp/ v. ★★★ parar *Stop talking and breathe.*

store /stɔr/ n. ★★★ loja *We can buy the tickets for the game at the sports store.*

stranger /ˈstreɪndʒər/ n. ★★ estranho, uma pessoa estranha *Children should never talk to strangers.*

strategy /ˈstrætədʒi/ n. ★★★ estratégia *The coach has a strategy to win the game.*

strawberry /ˈstrɔˌbɛri/ n. ★ morango *Strawberries are an excellent source of vitamins.*

street /strit/ n. ★★★ rua *Fourth Street is very dangerous at night.*

stress /strɛs/ n. ★★★ letra forte; sílaba tônica *The stress is on the last syllable.*

study /ˈstʌdi/ v. ★★★ estudar *I study with my friends every Wednesday.*

subject /ˈsʌbˌdʒɛkt/ n. ★★★ matéria **school subject** matéria escolar *Math is Jane's favorite subject.*

subtract /səbˈtrækt/ v. subtrair *Subtract 2 from 8 and you have 6.*

subway /ˈsʌbˌweɪ/ n. ★★ metrô *Do you take the bus or the subway to go to school?*

success /səkˈsɛs/ n. ★★★ sucesso *A hit is a momentaneous success.*

such /sʌtʃ/ det. pron. ★★★ tal *He is such a nice friend!*

sugar /ˈʃʊgər/ n. ★★★ açúcar *Harry likes his coffee with sugar.*

suggest /səgˈdʒɛst/ v. ★★★ sugerir *Suggest three songs for me to listen to.* **suggestion** sugestão

summarize /ˈsʌməˌraɪz/ v. ★ resumir *Summarize the text in three sentences.*

sure /ʃʊr/ adj. ★★★ claro, certo *I am sure he is at school.*

survey /ˈsɜrˌveɪ/ n. ★★★ pesquisa, enquete *We will do a survey about hobbies at school.*

sweat /swɛt/ v. n. ★ suar; suor *She sweats a lot when exercising.*

sweet /swit/ adj. ★★★ doce *Chocolate is Becky's favorite sweet.*

T

table /ˈteɪb(ə)l/ n. ★★★ mesa *The book is on the table.*

talented /ˈtæləntəd/ adj. ★ talentoso *Dave is a talented singer.*

talk /tɔk/ v. ★★★ falar *Talk to a classmate about your favorite hobbies.*

taste /teɪst/ n. ★★★ gosto, sabor *The taste of this dessert is excellent!*

teach /titʃ/ v. ★★★ ensinar *My brother and my uncle teach at the same school.*

teacher /ˈtitʃər/ n. ★★★ professor *Our teacher lives near the school.*

team /tim/ n. ★★★ time *They play on a handball team.*

teenager /ˈtinˌeɪdʒər/ n. ★★ adolescente *Lee is fourteen; he is a teenager.*

tell /tɛl/ v. ★★★ dizer *Tell me the truth.*

tend /tɛnd/ v. ★★★ tender *This type of rain tends to turn into a storm.*

test /tɛst/ n. ★★★ teste *We have a math test on Tuesday.*

text /tɛkst/ n. ★★★ texto *Read the text and answer the questions.*

than /ðæn/ conj. prep. ★★★ do que (comparativo) *He is taller than me.*

thank /θæŋk/ v. ★★★ agradecer *Thank your mother for the cake.*

thanks /θæŋks/ interj. ★★★ obrigado *Thanks for your answer.*

thanksgiving /ˈθæŋksˌgɪvɪŋ/ n. Dia de Ação de Graças (feriado americano) *In the US they have a special meal for Thanksgiving.*

then /ðɛn/ adj. adv. ★★★ então, em seguida *I brush my teeth, then I go to bed.*

there /ðɛr/ adj. inter. pron. ★★★ lá *My uncle lives over there.*

thing /θɪŋ/ n. ★★★ coisa *Friendship is the best thing in life.*

third /θɜrd/ numb. terceiro *Monique is the third of five children.*

thoughtful /ˈθɔtf(ə)l/ adj. ★ pensativo *Susan is really thoughtful today.*

through /θru/ adj. adv. prep. ★★★ por entre, por meio de *I can see through that window.*

throw /θroʊ/ v. ★★★ lançar, jogar *Throw the ball into the basket and score a point.*

ticket /ˈtɪkɪt/ n. ★★★ entrada, convite, bilhete *I have two tickets for the play.*

tidy up phrasal verb arrumar *I like to tidy up my bedroom.*

time /taɪm/ n. ★★★ tempo *We have time for a coffee.*

toast /toʊst/ n. ★ torrada *Toast with butter is healthy and delicious.*

tomorrow /təˈmɔroʊ/ adv. ★★★ amanhã *Today is Thursday; tomorrow is Friday.*

tongue twister expression trava-língua *It is hard but fun to say tongue twisters.*

too /tu/ adv. ★★★ também (usado no fim da frase) *You love me and I love you too.*

tooth /tuθ/ n. ★★★ dente *Adults generally have thirty-two teeth.* **toothbrush** escova de dente **toothpaste** pasta de dente **toothpick** palito de dente

touch /tʌtʃ/ v. ★★★ tocar *Stretch your arms and try to touch your toes.*

toy /tɔɪ/ n. ★★ brinquedo *Dolls are traditional toys.*

train /treɪn/ n. ★★★ trem *This train leaves at midnight.*

training /ˈtreɪnɪŋ/ n. ★★★ treinamento *We attend intensive training before the day of the competition.*

transfer /trænsˈfɜr/ v. ★★★ transferir *René needs to transfer some money from one account to another.*

trash /træʃ/ n. ★ lixo *This is trash, put it in the trash can.*

travel /ˈtræv(ə)l/ v. ★★★ viajar *Let's travel to Maceió.*

treat /trit/ v. ★★★ tratar *You should treat older people nicely.*

tree /tri/ n. ★★★ árvore *Let's rest under the tree.*

trip /trɪp/ n. ★★ viagem *This trip will take about seven hours.*

troop /trup/ n. ★★★ tropa *The troops will return home next season.*

try /traɪ/ v. ★★★ tentar *They will try to learn Chinese!*

turn /tɜrn/ v. girar, virar **turn on** ligar **turn off** desligar *Turn left at the next corner.*

twice /twaɪs/ adv. ★★★ duas vezes *I have swimming classes twice a week.*

twin /twɪn/ n. adj. ★★ gêmeo *Michael has a twin brother.*

Minidictionary

U

umbrella /ʌmˈbrelə/ n. ★ sombrinha, guarda chuva Take your umbrella; it's raining.

uncle /ˈʌŋk(ə)l/ n. ★★ tio My uncle is my dad's brother.

under /ˈʌndər/ adv. prep. ★★★ sob There is a ball under my bed.

underline /ˌʌndərˈlaɪn/ v. ★★ sublinhar Underline the answers in the text.

understand /ˌʌndərˈstænd/ v. entender Do you understand the question?

university /ˌjunɪˈvɜrsəti/ n. ★★★ universidade After high school, I want to go to the university.

unscramble /ʌnˈskræmb(ə)l/ v. desembaralhar Unscramble the words to form sentences.

until /ənˈtɪl/ conj. prep. ★★★ até I will stay here until you go to sleep.

use /juz/ v. ★★★ usar Use a pen to write your answers. **user** usuário

usually /ˈjuʒuəli/ adv. ★★★ geralmente My brother usually washes his car at home.

V

variety /vəˈraɪəti/ n. ★★★ variedade In Brazil, there is a great variety of kinds of banana.

vegetable /ˈvedʒ(ə)təb(ə)l/ n. ★★★ vegetal Lettuce is a common vegetable in salads. **vegetarian** vegetariano

very /ˈveri/ adj. adv. ★★★ muito This movie is very interesting.

veterinarian /ˌvet(ə)rɪˈneriən/ n. veterinário Nancy is a veterinarian because she likes to take care of animals.

vinegar /ˈvɪnɪɡər/ n. vinagre Fernando loves vinegar on his salad.

vinyl /ˈvaɪn(ə)l/ n. vinil In the past records discs used to be made of vinyl.

visit /ˈvɪzɪt/ v. ★★★ visitar Carina visits her grandparents every weekend. **visitor** visitante

visualize /ˈvɪʒuəˌlaɪz/ v. visualizar Open the software to visualize the text.

vitality /vaɪˈtæləti/ n. vitalidade My grandfather is 80 years old, but has a lot of vitality.

vocabulary /voʊˈkæbjəˌleri/ n. ★ vocabulário Let's learn some words and improve our vocabulary.

voice /vɔɪs/ n. ★★★ voz I heard his voice before he enters the room.

W

wait /weɪt/ v. ★★★ esperar Wait a minute, please.

wake up phrasal verb acordar Raquel wakes up at 6 o'clock.

walk /wɔk/ v. ★★★ andar I walk to school every day.

wall /wɔl/ n. ★★★ parede Post your compositions on the classroom wall.

want /wɑnt/ v. ★★★ querer I want to travel to China.

wash /wɑʃ/ v. ★★★ lavar Wash the dishes, please.

watch /wɑtʃ/ v. ★★★ ver, assistir Dorothy and Ron only watch TV only on the weekends.

way /weɪ/ n. ★★★ caminho, via This way is shorter than on the main road.

wealthy /ˈwelθi/ adj. ★★★ rico Luxembourg is considered a wealthy country.

wear /wer/ v. ★★★ vestir These teenagers wear uniform to school.

weight /weɪt/ n. ★★★ peso We use kilos and grams as a measure of weight.

welcome /ˈwelkəm/ v. n. ★★★ receber, bem-vindo Welcome to your new school!

well /wel/ adv. ★★★ bem Charlene speaks Italian very well.

what /wɑt/ adv. det. inter. pron. ★★★ o que What is your name?

when /wen/ adv. conj. ★★★ quando When is your birthday?

which /wɪtʃ/ deter. ★★★ qual Which cap do you prefer?

whistle /ˈwɪs(ə)l/ n. ★ assovio When you hear the whistle of a policeman, stop.

white /waɪt/ n. ★★★ branco White is the color of the clouds.

who /hu/ pron. ★★★ quem Who is your favorite singer?

why /waɪ/ adv. ★★★ por que Why do dogs bark?

wife /waɪf/ n. ★★ esposa My father's wife is Portuguese.

will /wɪl/ modal ★★★ indica tempo futuro They will travel next year.

window /ˈwɪndoʊ/ n. ★★★ janela This room has a glass window.

wine /waɪn/ n. ★★★ vinho People say a glass of wine a day is good for your health.

winner /ˈwɪnər/ n. ★★★ vencedor The winner receives a trophy at the end of the competition.

with /wɪθ/ prep. ★★★ com I live with my mom and my sister.

woman /ˈwʊmən/ n. ★★★ mulher Alice is a woman's name.

wonder /ˈwʌndər/ v. ★★★ imaginar I wonder if Wilson is in town today.

wood /wʊd/ n. ★★★ madeira This chair is made of wood.

word /wɜrd/ n. ★★★ palavra I is a very short word.

work /wɜrk/ v. ★★★ trabalho Flight attendants can work up to 18 hours a day.

world /wɜrld/ n. ★★★ mundo We want to guarantee our children a safer world.

would /wʊd/ modal ★★★ gostaria I would like a glass of water.

wrestling /ˈres(ə)lɪŋ/ n. luta livre esportiva Wrestling is a popular sport in Brazil.

write /raɪt/ v. ★★★ escrever I always write emails to my friends.

wrong /rɔŋ/ adj. ★★★ errado What is not correct is wrong.

Y

yawn /jɔn/ v. ★ bocejar People yawn when they are sleepy or bored.

year /jɪr/ n. ★★★ ano This is the year 2014.

yogurt /ˈjoʊɡərt/ n. iogurte Carina loves yogurt with passion fruit.

young /jʌŋ/ adj. ★★★ jovem My cousin is really young, he is 7 years old.

Website references

Page 14   **QMS.bc.ca** <http://www.qms.bc.ca/pages/boarding/daily-experience/>. Accessed April 2012.

Page 29   **ScienceDaily.com** <www.sciencedaily.com/releases/2009/02/090207150518.htm>. Accessed April 2012.

Page 32   **CampanhaDoAgasalho.sp.gov.br** <www.campanhadoagasalho.sp.gov.br>. Accessed April 2012.

Page 39   **SongLyrics.com** <www.songlyrics.com/avant/material-things-lyrics/>. Accessed April 2012.

Page 45   **KidsHealth.org** <kidshealth.org/kid/stay_healthy/food/breakfast.html>. Accessed April 2012.

Page 50   **Newton.dep.anl.gov** <www.newton.dep.anl.gov/askasci/bio99/bio99738.htm>. Accessed November 2011.

Page 57   **Gurl.com** <www.gurl.com/findout/hmh/qa/0,,626593,00.html>. Accessed November 2011.

Page 61   **Gargles.net** <http://gargles.net/evolution-of-the-toothbrush/>. Accessed November 2011.

DiscoveriesInMedicine.com <www.discoveriesinmedicine.com/To-Z/Toothbrush-and-Toothpaste.html>. Accessed November 2011.

BritishMuseum.org <www.britishmuseum.org/explore/families_and_children/museum_explorer/roman_britain/daily_life/grooming_tools.aspx>. Accessed November 2011.

Abc.net.au <www.abc.net.au/science/articles/2001/03/30/268342.htm>. Accessed November 2011.

DocShop.com <www.docshop.com/2008/04/07/the-causes-of-halitosis-and-how-to-remedy-bad-breath>. Accessed November 2011.

Page 68   **Garfield.com** <www.garfield.com/comics/vault.html?yr=1979&addr=790102>. Accessed December 2011.

Page 72   **TimeandDate.com** <www.timeanddate.com/worldclock>. Accessed November 2011.

SealandSerpent.org <www.sealandserpent.org/schedgen/schedulegenerator.php>. Accessed November 2011.

PsaResearch.com <http://www.psaresearch.com/. Accessed November 2011.

Page 73   **Cuisinenet.com** <www.cuisinenet.com/digest/breakfast/map_world.shtml>. Accessed November 2011.

DailyMotion.com <www.dailymotion.com/video/xehqz2_how-to-make-homemade-cheese_lifestyle>. Accessed November 2011.

AskDrM.org <http://askdrm.org/>. Accessed November 2011.

ItesLJ.org <iteslj.org/v/ei/body.html>. Accessed November 2011.

Page 95   **Brasil.gov.br** <www.brasil.gov.br/sobre/citizenship/urban-digital-cordiality/good-manners-in-society-1/br_model1?set_language=en>. Accessed April 2011.

Page 108 **GoBrazil.about.com** <gobrazil.about.com/od/tripplanning/ht/collectcall.htm>. Accessed December 2011.

Page 116 **Ecolocalizer.com** <ecolocalizer.com/2008/09/22/five-green-ways-to-dispose-of-that-old-cell-phone/>. Accessed December 2011.

Page 121 **News.BBC.co.uk** <http://news.bbc.co.uk>. Accessed December 2011.

Page 124 **HowToDrawGraffiti.net** <http://www.howtodrawgraffiti.net>. Accessed December 2011.

Page 125 **Educacao.UOL.com.br** <http://educacao.uol.com.br>. Accessed December 2011.

Page 133 **Books.google.com** <http://books.google.com/books>. Accessed December 2011.

Page 136 **Nces.ed.gov** <http://nces.ed.gov/nceskids/createagraph/default.aspx>. Accessed December 2011.

LearnEnglishKids.BritishCouncil.org <http://learnenglishkids.britishcouncil.org/en/tongue-twisters>. Accessed November 2011.

SoundCloud.com <http://soundcloud.com>. Accessed November 2011.

Page 137 **E-lixo.org** <http://www.e-lixo.org/>. Accessed December 2011.

MuseeVirtuel-VirtualMuseum.ca <http://www.museevirtuel-virtualmuseum.ca/index-eng.jsp>. Accessed December 2011.

Bibliography

BAKHTIN, M.; VOLOCHINOV, V. N. *Marxismo e filosofia da linguagem.* 11. ed. São Paulo: Hucitec, 2004.

BAWARSHI, A.; DEVITT, A.; REIFF, M. J. *Scenes of Writing: Strategies for Composing with Genres.* New York: Pearson Longman, 2004.

BAZERMAN, C. *Gêneros textuais, tipificação e interação.* São Paulo: Cortez, 2005.

BRASIL. Secretaria de Educação Fundamental. *Parâmetros curriculares nacionais: terceiro e quarto ciclos do Ensino Fundamental: língua estrangeira moderna.* Brasília: MEC, 1998.

BROWN, H. D. Teaching by Principles: *An Interactive Approach to Language Pedagogy.* New York: Pearson, 2001.

COSCARELLI, V. C.; RIBEIRO, A. E. *Letramento digital: aspectos sociais e possibilidades pedagógicas.* Belo Horizonte: Ceale / Autêntica, 2007.

FREIRE, P. *Pedagogia da autonomia: saberes necessários à prática educativa.* São Paulo: Paz e Terra, 1996.

GOWER, R.; PHILLIPS, D.; WALTERS, S. *Teaching Practice. A Handbook for Teachers in Training.* Oxford: Macmillan, 1995.

HARMER, J. *How to Teach English: An Introduction to the Practice of English Language Teaching.* Harlow: Pearson Longman, 2007.

HERNANDEZ, F.; VENTURA, M. *Organização do Currículo por Projetos de Trabalho. O Conhecimento e um Caleidoscópio.* Porto Alegre: Artmed, 1998

JOHNSON, K.; MORROW, K. *Communication in the Classroom.* Harlow: Pearson, 1990.

KLEIMAN, A. B.; MORAES, S. E. *Leitura e interdisciplinaridade: tecendo redes nos projetos da escola.* Campinas: Mercado de Letras, 1999.

KRESS, Gunther. *Reading Images: Multimodality, Representation and New Media*. Disponível em: <www.knowledgepresentation.org/BuildingTheFuture/Kress2/Kress2.html>. Accessed: 12 dez. 2006.

MEHISTO, P.; MARSH, D.; FRIGOLS, M. J. *Uncovering CLIL: Content and Language Integrated Learning in Bilingual and Multilingual Education*. Oxford: Macmillan, 2008.

MEURER, J. L.; BONINI, A.; MOTTA-ROTH, D. (Org.). *Gêneros: teorias, métodos, debates*. São Paulo: Parábola Editorial, 2005.

NUNAN, D. *Task-Based Language Teaching*. Cambridge: CUP, 2004.

RAJAGOPALAN, K. *Por uma linguística crítica: linguagem, identidade e a questão ética*. São Paulo: Parábola Editorial, 2003.

SCHNEUWLY, B.; DOLZ, J.; HALLER, S. *Gêneros orais e escritos na escola*. Trad. e org. ROJO, R. H. R.; CORDEIRO, G. S. Campinas: Mercado de Letras, 2004.

SCRIVENER, J. *Learning Teaching*. Oxford: Macmillan, 2004.

SIGNORINI, I.; CAVALCANTI, M. C. (Org.). *Linguística aplicada e transdisciplinaridade*. Campinas: Mercado de Letras, 2004.

TANNER, R.; GREEN C. *Tasks for Teacher Education: A Reference Approach Coursebook*. Harlow: Longman, 1998.

THORNBURY, S.; SLADE, D. *Conversation: From Description to Pedagogy*. Cambridge: CUP, 2006.

UR, P. *A Course in Language Teaching: Practice and theory*. Cambridge: CUP, 2001.

When and how to use your DVD-ROM

Multimedia Content 1 – Telling the time

When to use	Before activity 4, page 17 (Unit 1)
Content	Hours
Purpose	To practice telling the time in English.
What to do	Type the numbers in the digital watch according to the time you hear and see on the analogical watch.
Tips	Try to get used to telling the time both on digital and analogical watches (the ones that have pointers).

Multimedia Content 2 – My routine

When to use	At the end of page 33 (Unit 2)
Content	Describing routine activities
Purpose	To review the Simple Present (3rd person singular).
What to do	Relate the pictures to their respective descriptions.
Tips	Adapt the sentences to your reality. How would you give the same information about your routine? What would change in the sentences? What would change in the verbs?

Multimedia Content 3 – Breakfast

When to use	After activity 4, page 45 (Unit 3)
Content	Information about breakfast items
Purpose	To give more information about bread, butter, coffee, and milk.
What to do	Go through the infographic and learn more about the items mentioned above.
Tips	Infographics (*info* from information and *graphics* because of image use) help us understand a text by explaining it in a simple, visual, and attractive way.

Multimedia Content 4 – Brushing your teeth

When to use	After activity 1, page 61 (Unit 4)
Content	Video explaining how to brush your teeth
Purpose	To show how to brush teeth correctly.
What to do	Watch the video and compare it with how you brush your teeth.
Tips	Bring a toothbrush and toothpaste inside your pencil case. You spend a big part of your day at school, and it is important to have good dental hygiene during this period.

Multimedia Content 5 – Body tricks

When to use	After activity 2, page 80 (Unit 5)
Content	Infographics about tricks for the body.
Purpose	To give extra information about tricks for the body.
What to do	Go through the infographics and find out interesting information about tricks for the body.
Tips	Just like skin and eye color, these genetic features do not represent any kind of evolutive superiority or something similar. We are only human beings.

	Multimedia Content 6 – A tongue twister
When to use	After activity 3, page 87 (Unit 5)
Content	Tongue twisters
Purpose	To repeat tongue twisters in different ways in order to master saying them.
What to do	Listen and practice the rhythm in this tongue twister.
Tips	First listen to the complete sentence. Then listen to each part starting from the end. Once you can say each part separately, you should be able to say the whole sentence.

	Multimedia Content 7 – Do you have good manners?
When to use	After activity 3, page 93 (Unit 6)
Content	Quiz about good manners
Purpose	To test your knowledge about good manners.
What to do	Answer the questions honestly and find out whether you have good manners.
Tips	The purpose of this kind of quiz is not to score or win, but to learn more about yourself. That is why it is important to answer it honestly without thinking which answer would be more appropriate or would make you get a better score.

	Multimedia Content 8 – Culture: Holidays & celebrations: Thanksgiving
When to use	Before *Writing*, page 99 (Unit 6)
Content	Infographics about Thanksgiving Day
Purpose	To give information about this holiday: origin, habits, and trivia.
What to do	Read the information attentively observing the pictures to help comprehension.
Tips	Thanksgiving is also celebrated in Brazil. Article 1, Law no 781, from August 17, 1949, declares: "Single article. The National Day of Thanksgiving is established and shall be celebrated on the last Thursday in November." It was signed by President Gaspar Dutra; the date was changed in 1966 for "the fourth Thursday" to coincide with most of the celebrations worldwide.

	Multimedia Content 9 – Telephone conversations
When to use	Before *Listening*, page 111 (Unit 7)
Content	Game with telephone conversations
Purpose	To put some phone conversations in a logical order.
What to do	Read the lines in the balloons and continue the phone conversation appropriately.
Tips	Think of the logical sequence in a conversation: identifying the caller, the purpose of the call, hanging up.

	Multimedia Content 10 – Graffiti
When to use	While doing *Crossroads* da page 124 (Unit 8)
Content	Graffiti simulator
Purpose	To create a personal tag (stylized signature).
What to do	Use the simulator to create a personal tag.
Tips	Graffiti techniques may also be used in paper. Respect private property. Law number 12,408 regulates graffiting and prohibits spray paint sales to minors.

Capa: Getty Images: Mario Goldman/AFP (geleira) Eric Delmar/Getty Images (balões) Eric Raptosh Photography/Getty Images (quarto)

Imagens cedidas por **Solveig Barlow** 120, 121

Imagens do livro Where Children Sleep 24, 25, 26, 27, 33 **by James Mollison, published by Chris Boot** © James Mollison / Chris Boot Ltd

Imagem do British Museum 61 **©The Trustees of the British Museum. All rights reserved.**

Projeto em origami executado por **Karen Tiemy Ohara** 105

Arquivo pessoal da autora 53

Bigstock: Bigstock 12

Getty Images: Andersen Ross 107, Hans Neleman 88, Rick Diamond 38 (Avant), SambaPhoto/Marcelo Reis 118 (Drummond), Seymour Hewitt 54, Simone Mueller 106, Getty Images 79 (língua e imã), 81 (boca), 85 (estalar), 95 (ônibus), 97, 98 (porta), 99 (sala), 103 (todas menos mural, mensagem, mulher chorando e homem abrindo a porta), 109 (botões), 111 (rapaz de olho claro ao telefone), 114 (2g), 80 (língua dobrada)

Shutterstock: 1000 Words 119 (amarelinha), aceshot1 141 (ônibus), action studio 122 (teatro), Adriano Castelli 123 (fotos), AISPIX 141 (Ryan), AJP 43 (prato de baixo), Allison Achauer 128 (2), Allonzo Inc 130, Amy Myers 15 (futebol), Andrea Haase 127 (2-pintura), Andrey Shadrin 115, Anetta 16 (comer), Anton Prado PHOTO 47 (café), Ardelean Andreea 122 (grafiteiro), Argunova 46 (cereal), Arno Jenkins 30 (mp3 player), atoss 46 (xícara), AYAKOVLEV 122 (2 bailarinos), azhuvalappil 48 (limão), Barone Firenze 29 (videogame), Beata Becla 35 (livros), bezikus 30, 31 (camelo), Billy Alexander 3, 12, 24, 42, 54, 76, 88, 106, 118 (fundo), Black Rock Digital 113 (2a), Blazej Lyjak 145 (a), Blend Images 147 (b), bloody 138 (c), bonchan 30 (comida), 46 (frutas), CandyBox Images 148 (1-direita), Catalin Petolea 147 (c), Chad McDermott 103 (homem abrindo a porta), Charles Amundson 141 (basquete), Christi Tolbert 145 (e), Christina Richards 134, CLKER 108 (ícones telefônicos), Copestello 131 (5), corepics 122 (fotografo), criben 122 (atores), Cristi Lucaci 114 (2f), CYC 122 (paisagem), dakolix 30 (jeans), Denis Dryashkin 46 (maçã), Denis Pepin 122 (designer), dipego 131 (1), Dmitriy Aseev 116, Dmitriy Shironosov 139 (e), Drimi 127 (2-pescultura), Dusan Jankovic 146 (e), EasyEstereogramBuilder.com 131 (6), Ecelop 138 (food, a, b), Edyta Pawlowska 148 (2), ejwhite 15 (dois meninos), Elena Elisseeva 114 (2e), Elena Itsenko 30 (maquiagem), elena moiseeva 42 (prato de baixo), Elzbieta Sekowska 43 (prato de cima), euko 141 (matemática), EuToch 46 (queijo), Evgeny Karandaev 46 (copo), eyespeak 19 (meninos), Faraways 46 (chá), forestpath 147 (e), fotoluminate 147 (f), gillmar 8 (ovos), Goodluz 15 (sala de aula), gosphotodesign 146 (a), graja 146 (d), httpKzenon 139 (a), Iakov Filimonov 28 (meninas), iconspro 6, 33 (ícone), ifong 46, 50 (leite), ilker canikligil 30 (celular), J. Henning Buchholz 28 (celular), jaddingt 3 (mala), Jenny Leonard 119 (escadaria), jocic 28 (tênis), jordache 16 (estudar), Jorg Hackemann 123 (dinossauro), Josep Pena Llorens 30 (elefante), Joseph Calev 50 (sal), Josh Resnick 47 (torradas), jreika 42 (prato de cima), Julija Sapic 139 (f), Kameel4u 15 (acordar), Karkas 28 (jaqueta), Konstantin Sutyagin 139 (c), kristian stokholm 129 (a), Kshishtof 122 (grafite), Kurhan 146 (b), Lena.Le. 47 (bolacha com geleia), Lisa F. Young 145 (d), Lorraine Kourafas 47 (omelete), Losevsky Pavel 122 (banda), Luis Stortini Sabor aka CVA 131 (2), Lusoimages 46 (bolo), M. Unal Ozmen 50 (farinha), Maggie Ayame 103 (lápis), Mahesh Patil 138 (d), maigi 122 (fotos), Marijus Auruskevicius 18 (lousa), Mark Hayes 145 (b), Mark William Penny 124 (try), Maxim Petrichuk 29 (ski), Mehmet Dilsiz 16 (chegada), michaeljung 146 (c), Michal Zacharzewski 49 (pães), mikeledray 111 (menino no telefone público), 114 (2c), Mircea BEZERGHEANU 122 (construção), Moi Cody 129 (b), Monkey Business Images 139 (b), Morgan Lane Photography 15 (família), Muellek Josef 29 (elefantes), Nagy Melinda 40 (fotos cavalo), Natalia Belotelova 127 (2-prédio), Natalia Mylova 141 (jantar), Neale Cousland 30 (caminito), 122 (escultura), netbritish 15 (aula de computação), nito 47 (bolacha), Olaf Speier 122 (escultor), OlegDoroshin 122 (prédio desenhado), olly 122 (pintor), optimarc 134 (7), Orange Line Media 147 (d), OtnaYdur 141 (violão), Paul Maguire 15 (dormir), Pete Saloutos 145 (c), Peteri 131 (4), picamaniac 47 (geleia), pio3 135 (5,6,8 p preto), Pixel 4 Images 28 (show), Pixelspieler 50 (queijo limburger), pulsar75 46 (chocolate), pzAxe 114 (2d), ra2 studio 30 (tablet), Racheal Grazias 30 (parque de diversões), rea einskisdóttir 45 (cereal), riekephoto 147 (a), Robbi 14 (mural), Robert Milek 47 (pão), Sandra Gligorijevic 15 (duas crianças), Sandra P 135 (8-colorido), SeanPavonePhoto 141 (TV), Sergej Razvodovskij 29 (celular), Simon James 146 (f), Simon Smith 124 (tag), sippakorn 111 (moça de franja), Slava Gerj 127 (2-crânio), Slaven 122 (desenhista, poema), snowblurred 128 (1-menino), Stephen Coburn 48 (menina), Stuart Monk 34 (menino), Supri Suharjoto 111 (moça de cabelo preto), 113 (2b), 139 (d), 148 (1-esquerda), Svyatoslav Palenyy 129 (c), SXC 78, 87, Tamara Kulikova 145 (a), Tatiana Popova 122 (partitura), Thomas Barrat 28 (balão), Timur Djafarov 124 (piece), Tischenko Irina 46 (banana, pão de forma), Tobik 46 (pão francês, presunto), toonman 37 (turma), Tracy Whiteside 122 (porta), Trish 30 (mini game), upstudio 23 (agenda), Valentyn Volkov 47 (leite), vermicule 131 (3), Vjom 20, 32, 48, 80, 97, 126, 149 a 152 (carinhas), Volodymyr Krasyuk_B 50 (queijo), winnond 27 (campainha), Winston Link 21 (tapete), Yevgenia Gorbulsky 118 (janela), 18 (cereal, menino), 48 (casal), 48 (mulheres), 48 (menino), 111 (moça de blusa roxa), 123 (pinturas), Shutterstock 51, 52, 56 (todas menos menino), 57, 58 (todas menos mãos cruzadas e escovando os dentes), 59, 60, 61 (todas menos utensílios antigos), 62, 63 (todas menos cachorro, menino sujo e metrô), 65 (todas menos xícara), 67, 69, 70 (sabonete e enxágue bucal), 72, 73, 74 (robô), 75, 76, 77, 79 (todas menos língua e imã), 80 (todas menos menino e língua dobrada), 81 (todas menos boca), 84 (mural), 85 (todas menos estalar e menino olho virado), 86, 91, 95 (lixo e homem), 96, 99 (biblioteca e mensagem), 100 (desenhos), 101, 102, 104, 112, 122 (bailarinas)

Thinkstock: Comstock 111 (meninos na cozinha), Creatas 80 (menino), Digital Vision 111 (menino no sofá ao telefone), Goodshoot 127 (1), Hemera 17, 141 (computador), 142, iStockphoto 8 (mala), 18 (sala de aula), 26 (mapa), 37 (fruta), 47 (manteiga), 47 (pão com manteiga), 56 (menino), 58 (mãos cruzadas; escovando os dentes), 103 (mural, mulher chorando e mensagem), 111 (mulher de azul ao telefone), 124 (BiY!), 124 (frase), 128 (1-mulheres), 138 (canguru), Photodisc 50 (bacteria), 98 (avião), photos.com 30 (guitarra), ryan McVay 16 (violão), Stockbyte 85 (menino olho virado), Zoonar 47 (café com leite), Thinkstock 63 (cachorro, menino sujo e metrô), 65 (xícara), 70 (xampu, desodorante e pasta de dente), 74 (jovens).

O **Macmillan Dictionary** foi usado como referência na produção do Minidictionary.

Todos os direitos reservados. Nenhuma parte desta publicação pode ser reproduzida, estocada por qualquer sistema ou transmitida por quaisquer meios ou formas existentes ou que venham a ser criados, sem prévia permissão por escrito da Editora.

Este material contém links para sites de terceiros. Não controlamos ou nos responsabilizamos pelos conteúdos destes sites. Favor usar de cautela ao acessá-los.

Todos os esforços foram feitos no sentido de encontrar os detentores dos direitos das obras protegidas por copyright. Caso tenha havido alguma omissão involuntária, os editores terão o maior prazer em corrigi-la na primeira oportunidade.

O material de publicidade e propaganda reproduzido nesta obra está sendo utilizado única e exclusivamente para fins didáticos, não representando qualquer tipo de recomendação de produtos ou empresas por parte dos autores e da editora.

Há reproduções de artigos de revistas ou jornais em que são mencionadas pessoas reais. Seus nomes foram mantidos, porém, suas fotos foram substituídas para preservar suas imagens.

As fotos / imagens que não constam desta relação têm seus créditos na página onde aparecem em razão de exigências contratuais.

Agradecimentos

Gostaríamos de expressar nossos agradecimentos às pessoas que nos acompanharam ao longo desta jornada:
- às nossas famílias, pela compreensão e apoio incondicional, sem julgamentos ou críticas quanto às nossas escolhas profissionais;
- a todos os professores que passaram por nossas vidas e que inspiraram essa experiência magnífica de compartilhar conhecimentos;
- aos nossos amigos e colegas de trabalho, que nos proporcionaram aprendizados valiosos e conforto nos momentos difíceis da carreira;
- a todos os alunos, razão de nossa existência, por terem mantido acesa a chama do entusiasmo, dedicação e amor pelo ensino;
- e também a você, usuário deste livro. Desejamos que você tenha uma carreira tão gratificante e apaixonante quanto as nossas.

Obrigado!

Os autores.